MapleMoon™

a maple syrup cookbook

*North American natives called
the time of gathering maple syrup
the "Season of the Maple Moon".*

We call it spring.

by
Johanna (van der Zeijst) Bates

*Front Cover
Cornmeal Maple Waffles, page 20*

Maple Moon™– *a maple syrup cookbook*
by
Johanna (van der Zeijst) Bates

First Printing — June 2001

Copyright © 2001 by
Johanna M. Bates

Maple Moon Publishing
Suite 101, 2212 – 34th Ave. S.W.
Calgary, Alberta, Canada T2T 2C6

National Library of Canada Cataloguing in Publication Data

Bates, Johanna van der Zeijst, 1948 –
  Maple moon

  Includes index.
  ISBN 1-894022-63-7

1. Cookery (Maple sugar and syrup) I. Title.
TX767.M3B37 2001   641.6'364   C2001-910729-3

Linens courtesy of Edelweiss Village, Calgary, Alberta
China courtesy of Bowring, Calgary, Alberta
China courtesy of The Compleat Cook, Calgary, Alberta
China courtesy of The Royal Doulton Store, Calgary, Alberta

Photography by Ross Hutchinson, Hutchinson and Company, Calgary, Alberta
Cover Painting by William Roy Brownridge

Page formatting by Iona Glabus, PW Group
Cover Lettering and Colour Separations by Murray Timm, PW Group

Designed, Printed and Produced in Canada by:
Centax Books, A Division of PW Group
Publishing Director, Photo Designer and Food Stylist – Margo Embury
1150 Eighth Avenue, Regina, Saskatchewan, Canada S4R 1C0
(306) 525-2304   Fax: (306) 757-2439
centax@printwest.com   www.centaxbooks.com

Dedication

To my dearly beloved friends,
Mary Samide and Frank Johnson,
with gratitude for listening
long after I was boring myself to death.

Also thanks to Donna Scherbak, Beth Blair, Colin Logiss, Pat Appel, Terry Garvin, Janet Reardon, Paul and Susan Thompson, Dr. Chris Whittington, Jean Auger-Crowe, Connie Rosenstein, Hazel Corcoran, Bonnie Racz, master candy specialist Lynne Heninger, Shirley MacLeod, Colin McDonald, Wendy Lukasiewicz, Beth Duthie, Lori Lukasewich, Oney Martin, Eleanor Love and, of course, my beloved children, Matthew, Larissa, Raymond and Allan.

A great big hug of gratitude to Margo Embury . . . without you, Margo, nothing would happen.

Table of Contents

Maple Beverages, Breakfasts & Breads   7

Maple Soups, Salads, Vegetables & Sauces   29

Maple Main Course Dishes.   59

Maple & Fruit   85

Maple Candies & Puddings   107

Maple Pies   121

Maple Cakes, Squares & Cookies   135

Maple & Chocolate – Twin Passions   147

Resource Section   165

Index   167

These recipes have been tested in U. S. standard measurements. Common metric measurements are given as a convenience for those who are more familiar with metric. These recipes have not been tested in metric.

Maple
Beverages,
Breakfasts
&
Breads

The First Nations People and the Maple Tree

It has been suggested throughout the relatively short period of recorded North American history that the First Nations People did not actually know how to make pure maple syrup and, its derivative, maple sugar. In light of their in-depth knowledge of their environment, such a suggestion is totally ludicrous. Their world was their supermarket. Whenever I climb Nose Hill, the stark, windswept ancestral hunting grounds of the Blackfoot Nation in Alberta, I am in awe of the fact that they could live and thrive in -40° Celsius/Fahrenheit temperatures. I can't stay up there for an hour in those temperatures without running to the local latte shop.

The aboriginal people used all of nature's products for their daily nutrition and medicine. On the prairies, goldenrod was used for a dye; fall asters were used for medicinal purposes; willow fungus was used to relieve earache; during the fifties, seneca root dug on the great prairie was purchased by drug companies, ostensibly for use in dental offices as a component in freezing. Cattail root was used as a vegetable. It was also used as a thickener in the same way that we use cornstarch and tapioca or flour. The natives were similarly imaginative with the sap of the maple.

My mama and I were discussing the natives' intense desire for maple syrup and the fact that they added it to everything that they ate. Having lived in the Netherlands during the Second World War, she understood the natives perfectly. When rationing was on, she looked everywhere for a sweetener; there was no sugar to be had. Mama would travel great distances to farms and collect huge, old sugar beets from the farmers. She would cut these beets into chunks and boil them for hours, until some molasses eased out of them, then strain the end product through cloth to provide some sweetening. The entire process blackened my mother's hands and strained her wrists. All these years later my mother still turns her nose up at molasses. Mama is a *big* fan of maple syrup.

It is certain that the Iroquois Confederacy (the Mohawk, Seneca, Oneida, Onandaga and the Cayuga) as well as the Huron and Algonquin used maple syrup extensively in both liquid and solid form. An ancient Iroquois legend explained the genesis of the use of maple syrup. As with many discoveries, it was based on a lucky accident, the accidental insertion of a tomahawk in a tree. The Iroquois themselves celebrated the advent of the running of the syrup with a "maple dance".

The natives looked askance at the white sugar brought along by the settlers, calling it "French snow", and taught the Dutch, English and French settlers the secrets of the "maple moon". The maple moon usually began in early March and lasted until early to mid-April, depending on the weather. The flow of sap was a huge event and was celebrated with roughly the same vigour as Mardi Gras is in Western society. The women made gift baskets, *mokuks*, out of birch bark and elaborate gifts out of the maple cakes. These cakes were often huge, and the more artistic natives rendered the maple sugar into shapes that represented their passions and spirituality.

 8

The various Indian tribes boiled their sap in bark containers. When they saw the iron and copper kettles of the settlers and fur traders, they were intrigued. They traded generously for kettles in which to make their maple sugar. They quickly discovered that their log and bark containers, while absolutely desirable for canoes, were inferior to the European metal pots when it came to the production of maple sugar. In their excellent book, *The Maple Sugar Book*, Helen and Scott Nearing quote from W.J. Hoffman, writing in *The Menomini Indians*, Fourteenth Annual Report of the Bureau of Ethnology, (1896):

> *The Ojibwa . . . who number less than 1500, had, during the preceding spring, made almost ninety tons of sugar. When it is taken into consideration that nearly all of the sugar is consumed by the Indians themselves, it shows an almost abnormal fondness for sweets. It virtually forms a substitute for salt.*

This cook disagrees with Mr. Hoffman as to the "abnormal fondness for sweets". It may be over a hundred years later but anyone can tell you that a newborn baby will turn its head towards sweets. Not so with anything that is sour or salty. The urge for sweets is as old as mankind.

In fact, another indigenous people, the Inuit, loved sweets as much as the native tribes to the south. The Inuit lived above the tree line and had no access to maple syrup. They were however introduced to white sugar by the European settlers. In his book, *The Incredible Eskimo*, Father Raymond de Coccola described his ministry to the Inuit from 1933 to 1948. Part of his flock was accidentally exposed to a flu virus through a simple handshake. The Inuit had absolutely no immunity to the virus and Father Raymond nursed his dying friends. As one young friend, Naodluak, lay dying, he asked his beloved Father Raymond, "Fala (using the pet name that the Inuit had given the good priest), will there be a lot of sugar in the land of the good Spirit?" "Yes," said Father Raymond, "and many more joys than just sugar." With that assurance, Naodluak laid down his head and died with a smile on his face.

If eating EVERYTHING with maple syrup was good enough for the Ojibwa, the Hurons and the Iroquois, it's good enough for me. These tribes would often eat nothing but maple sugar cakes for weeks on end, and they thrived on it. Early settlers took their cue from the natives and believed in the medicinal properties of maple syrup as a cure for rheumatism.

The Maple Sugar Book details various methods of collection of maple sap through the ages. In their observations of the production of sap through the centuries, you can see that nothing really changes. The basic issue was always cost, as the independent colonist tried to maximize production to support the needs of large families. So, too, anyone who went into large-scale production was faced with basic challenges. Omnipresent was the need to collect as much sap as possible, use efficient piping systems and keep the maple sap clean during collection and storage. Notwithstanding all of the problems with the harvest, French soldiers in the forts and settlers, both French and English in Upper and Lower Canada, rigorously adhered to the practice of laying in an annual supply of maple syrup to satisfy both body and soul.

Maple Summer Sangria

This is the non-alcoholic version of the famous Spanish summer drink. You can call it Canada meets Spain in Alberta. I've been known to float wild roses in sangria because they look and smell so lovely, and they are the symbol of the province (remember to de-bug the roses first).

2 cups	freshly squeezed orange juice	500 mL
¼ cup	lemon juice (strained)	60 mL
4 cups	cranberry cocktail	1 L
½ cup	maple syrup	125 mL
2 cups	sliced or halved fresh strawberries	500 mL
1 cup	fresh blueberries	250 mL
1 cup	sliced fresh ripe peaches	250 mL
1 cup	sliced fresh mangoes	250 mL
1	orange, sliced	1
1	lemon	1
1 cup	maple sugar	250 mL
2 qts.	club soda	2 L

Mix all ingredients, except the last 3, in a glass punch bowl. Chill for about 5 hours. Before serving, squeeze the lemon and dip the rims of tall serving glasses in the juice. Then dip the glasses in the maple sugar to sugar-coat the rims. Add the club soda to the sangria and serve with ice.

Serves: 8

Variation: For a **Maple Wine Sangria**, just add 26 oz. (750 mL) of dry white wine to the Maple Summer Sangria.

Maple Mango Smoothie

This is a luxurious mango shake — it can also be a nutritious breakfast drink if you use milk or yogurt instead of ice cream.

4 cups	fresh mango chunks	1 L
1 cup	fresh mango juice	250 mL
½ cup	maple syrup	125 mL
2 qts.	vanilla ice cream	2 L
	club soda	

Maple Mango Smoothie
(continued)

Peel and pit enough mangoes to yield 4 cups (1 L) of pulp. In a food processor or blender, purée fresh mangoes and juice and add maple syrup. Blend completely. Slowly add the vanilla ice cream and blend until creamy. Fill glasses with this mango shake and then add the club soda to taste. Stir until smooth and creamy.

Serves: 6

Note: If you are dieting, substitute fat-free yogurt or skim milk for the ice cream and cut the calories substantially.

Variations: This smoothie recipe is very versatile. Substitute peaches, bananas or pineapple chunks for mango and try orange juice or pineapple juice instead of mango juice. Use your imagination and try your favourite flavour combinations.

Irish Canadian Coffee

The folks at Turkey Hill Sugarbush Ltd. frequently foam their milk for lattes and add a tablespoon (15 mL) of maple syrup. It creates a lovely maple froth. This recipe was provided as a holiday treat.

¼ cup	Irish whiskey OR Canadian whisky*	60 mL
1 tsp.	pure maple syrup	5 mL
	strong, freshly brewed coffee	
	whipped cream sweetened with maple syrup	

Combine the whiskey and maple syrup in a suitable glass or mug and fill it with coffee. Top with whipped cream. Relax and enjoy!!

* Whiskey or whisky? In Ireland and the U.S. it's spelled whiskey – in Canada and Scotland it's spelled whisky.

Serves: 1

11

Crunchy Maple Cranberry Granola

Maple syrup adds delicious sweetness to this healthy breakfast cereal, snack or dessert topping. Serve it with milk, eat it out of hand or sprinkle it generously over yogurt, ice cream or fresh fruit salads.

5 cups	rolled oats	1.25 L
1½ cups	flaked coconut	375 mL
½ cup	sesame seeds	125 mL
½ cup	sunflower seeds	125 mL
1 cup	wheat germ	250 mL
¾ cup	chopped almonds	175 mL
½ tsp.	cinnamon	2 mL
½ tsp.	nutmeg	2 mL
1 tsp.	salt	5 mL
¾ cup	maple syrup	175 mL
¾ cup	vegetable oil	175 mL
1 cup	dried cranberries	250 mL
½ cup	chopped dried apples OR apricots OR dried blueberries	125 mL

In a large roasting pan, combine the oats, coconut, sesame and sunflower seeds, wheat germ, almonds, cinnamon, nutmeg and salt. Combine maple syrup and oil and pour over the oat mixture. Stir thoroughly.

Temperature: 300°F (150°C)

Baking Time: 45 minutes to 1 hour – stir every 15 minutes

Remove the granola from the oven. Stir well. Cool and stir in the dried fruit. Store in an airtight container.

Yield: 10 cups (2.5 L) of granola

Magnificent Maple Granola

You can get really sick of prepared cereals and the same old, same old breakfast every day. If you prepare this ahead, you will have a breakfast to talk about for awhile, not to mention a treat to look forward to when you get up.

4 cups	rolled oats	1 L
2 cups	wheat flakes, long cooking	500 mL
1 cup	oat bran	250 mL
1 cup	sunflower seeds	250 mL
1 cup	pumpkin seeds	250 mL
1 cup	cashews	250 mL
½ cup	vegetable oil	125 mL
1 tbsp.	cinnamon	15 mL
¼ cup	maple sugar	60 mL
¾ cup	maple syrup	175 mL
1 cup	dark raisins	250 mL
¼ cup	chopped crystallized ginger	60 mL
½ cup	chopped candied mango	125 mL
¼ cup	chopped candied papaya	60 mL

Mix the rolled oats, wheat flakes, oat bran, sunflower seeds, pumpkin seeds and cashews in a large bowl. In a small saucepan, heat sunflower oil, cinnamon, maple sugar and maple syrup. Cook over low heat until the mixture can be easily poured. Pour the syrup mixture over the grain/nut combination and then scoop into a large cooking pan. (I use the same huge pan that I cook ribs in.) Bake on the middle oven rack.

Temperature: 225°F (110°C)

Baking Time: 2 to 2½ hours – stir every half hour or so.

When the granola is properly toasted, remove from the oven and stir in the raisins and candied fruit. Use during the next 2 weeks or so. Store in the refrigerator for optimum freshness.

Yield: 12 cups (3 L) of granola

Raymond's Mac Crêpes

This is my son Raymond's acronym for Maple, Apple and Cinnamon. Four children who love pancakes have resulted in a lot of early morning hours at the stove. The boys fight about who will get the "first pancake" on a Saturday or Sunday morning. Raymond recently said I should open up a restaurant and call it FIRST PANCAKE. In any event, these are a hit on Saturday morning.

6	Granny Smith apples, cored and sliced	6
1 cup	maple syrup	250 mL
½ cup	water	125 mL
1 tbsp.	cinnamon	15 mL
2 tbsp.	maple cream liqueur*	30 mL
4 tbsp.	unsalted butter	60 mL
10	prepared crêpes, kept warm (see Johnny's Skinny Pancakes on page 15)	10
¾ cup	chopped macadamia nuts	175 mL

Place the sliced apples, maple syrup, water and cinnamon in a saucepan. Bring to a boil and simmer until the apples are tender and the maple sauce has thickened. You want most of the liquid to evaporate and the timing will depend on what altitude you are at and what the humidity is in your neck of the woods. Add the maple cream liqueur and the butter towards the end, mixing well. Place crêpes on individual plates and spoon some of the apples into each crêpe. Pour a generous portion of sauce over apples and fold crêpes. Sprinkle with macadamia nuts and, while you're at it, throw some more maple syrup on top.

Serves: 5

* *If you are concerned about alcohol content, the maple liqueur all burns off in the heat and you are left with only the superb flavour.*

Pictured on page 17.

Johnny's Skinny Pancakes

These aren't really pancakes in the ordinary sense of the word. They are crêpes. My nephew John noted that I never made the North American-style thicker pancakes, and he called these "skinny pancakes" . . . hence the name. These crêpes have been made in our home every Saturday and Sunday morning for about 25 years. They are easy to make. Simply use a non-stick skillet, small or large, depending on taste. I purchase a new skillet every year or so, much to the horror of my mama. She says if I used plastic tools I'd scratch the surface less and I would never need a new pan. I'm taking it under advisement.

1 cup	all-purpose flour	250 mL
1½ cups	milk	375 mL
3	eggs	3
½ tsp.	salt	2 mL
3 tbsp.	butter	45 mL

Place all ingredients, except the butter, in a blender and blend for 30 seconds or so. Make sure the flour doesn't stick to the sides. Scrape down any excess flour and then blend again briefly.

Place the butter in a skillet and pour in just enough batter to cover the bottom. Cook until the sides of the crêpe lift up and you can flip it over. Cook until golden brown on each side. Repeat until all batter is used up. Serve immediately.

These crêpes can be stockpiled for a brunch. Cover with foil and warm in a 200°F (95°C) oven.

Serve with fruit, maple syrup, maple sugar and Maple Whipped Cream, as with the Maple Sugar Waffles on page 19.

Yield: 6 to 8 pancakes

Allan's Dutch Apple Baby

My son Allan is my youngest and, through a legal fluke, he is a citizen of The Netherlands, while his siblings aren't. He has had to fight hard for his pancakes as he lined up behind his older brothers and sister. This pancake is for him.

4 tbsp.	butter	60 mL
5	Granny Smith apples, cored, peeled and thinly sliced	5
¼ cup	brown sugar	60 mL
1 tsp.	cinnamon	5 mL
¼ cup	lemon juice	60 mL
1 cup	all-purpose flour	250 mL
1 cup	whole milk	250 mL
¼ cup	berry/superfine sugar	60 mL
¼ tsp.	salt	1 mL
3	large eggs	3
1 tbsp.	butter	15 mL
3 tbsp.	powdered sugar	45 mL
1 cup	maple syrup	250 mL

Heat a large, iron skillet. Melt butter and then add apples, brown sugar, cinnamon and lemon juice. Sauté for 5 to 7 minutes, until the apples are tender and the brown sugar has caramelized. Remove the apple mixture and all of the juices to a separate pan and keep warm.

Place the flour in a large mixing bowl. In a separate bowl or blender container, mix the milk, berry sugar, salt and eggs until all ingredients are well incorporated. Add the milk mixture to the flour and mix well. Heat the butter in the skillet and coat the bottom well, or spray the bottom of the pan with non-stick spray. Pour the batter into the pan. Add the apple mixture and bake.

Temperature: 425°F (220°C)

Baking Time: 20 minutes

Pour the maple syrup over the pancake and, finally, sprinkle the baked pancake with powdered sugar.

Serves: 4 adults or 2 teenagers

Note: You will need to use a heavy iron skillet for this recipe as the pancake bottom will burn if you use a "thin" pan.

Maple Sugar Waffles

Breakfast is the only meal of the day that can't possibly be missed. The remaining meals are just window dressing. If you are getting up to waffles, maple syrup and fruit, the leap out of bed is so much quicker. Make sure that you serve the waffles immediately. If you leave them in a slow oven, they will harden and be unpalatable. Your reputation will be ruined.

1 cup	all-purpose flour	250 mL
1 tbsp.	maple sugar	15 mL
1½ tsp.	baking powder	7 mL
1 tsp.	cinnamon*	5 mL
1 cup	buttermilk	250 mL
2	eggs	2
3 tbsp.	vegetable oil	45 mL
	non-stick cooking spray	

Place the flour, maple sugar, baking powder, baking soda, cinnamon, buttermilk, eggs and oil in a blender. Blend until well mixed. Scrape the sides to make sure all ingredients are incorporated.

Spray a preheated waffle iron with non-stick spray and pour in enough batter to cover the surface. Cook until the waffle separates easily from the iron. Spray the waffle iron again and continue cooking until your guests are happy.

Serve with maple syrup and fresh fruit – I prefer blueberries, mangoes, fresh lychee, raspberries or strawberries.

Yield: 8 waffles

* *If you aren't crazy about cinnamon, cut to ½ tsp. (2 mL) or eliminate completely. By personal choice the cinnamon flavour is very pronounced.*

Variation: If you want to serve these waffles with whipped cream, make **Maple Whipped Cream** by whipping 1 cup (250 mL) of cream with 3 tbsp. (45 mL) maple syrup or maple sugar. Add a dollop of whipped cream to the waffles and fruit.

Maple Gouda Soup, page 35

Cornmeal Maple Waffles

Our family loves the slightly gritty texture of cornmeal. It also adds flavour and a lovely golden colour to these super breakfast waffles.

1	extra large egg	1
¾ cup	whole milk	175 mL
¼ cup	vegetable oil	60 mL
1 cup	all-purpose flour	250 mL
3 tbsp.	cornmeal	45 mL
2 tsp.	baking powder	10 mL
1 tbsp.	maple sugar OR maple syrup	15 mL
¼ tsp.	salt	1 mL

Preheat waffle iron. Combine all ingredients in a blender and blend on MIX until all ingredients are moistened. Make sure nothing sticks to the sides. Spray the waffle iron with non-stick spray and pour ½ cup (125 mL) of batter onto the griddle. Close the waffle iron and bake until golden. Lift when the lid opens easily.

Waffles take 2 to 3 minutes to bake. Serve hot with your favourite seasonal fruit and maple syrup.

Yield: 8 waffles

Variation: For **Cornmeal Waffles with Bacon**, cut very thin slices of raw bacon in half and lay them on top of the batter in the waffle iron. Close the waffle iron and bake and serve as above.

Pictured on the front cover.

Raymond's Hurry-Up/ Wake-Up Maple Bananas

My son frequently steals those last few minutes in bed before school or work and then pays the price in lack of time. This is his maple creation. He says it's nutritious, delicious and can be made in seconds, so it fits in with most teenage lifestyles. He's right. In terms of "fast food", he could do a lot worse.

| 2 | bananas, peeled and sliced down the middle but not split entirely through
peanut butter, crunchy or plain and as much as you like
maple syrup, as much as you like | 2 |

Spread peanut butter in the cavities of the bananas, as though you were spreading mustard on a hot dog bun. Pour maple syrup along the peanut butter groove and eat on the run. Take a napkin along in case of leakage.

Serves: 2

Note: Bananas are great nutrition in a user-friendly package. Rich in potassium and a good source of Vitamin C, they are also high carbohydrate, relatively low fat and they satisfy your appetite.

You can speed up the ripening process by putting bananas in a partially open or perforated brown paper bag.

Maple Glory Muffins

These are great for breakfast! If you hate mornings, it makes getting up worthwhile!

2 cups	all-purpose flour	500 mL
1½ cups	maple syrup	375 mL
1 tbsp.	baking soda	15 mL
2 tsp.	cinnamon	10 mL
1 tsp.	salt	5 mL
3	large eggs	3
1 cup	vegetable oil	250 mL
1 tbsp.	maple cream liqueur OR maple liqueur	15 mL
2 cups	zucchini	500 mL
¾ cup	raisins	175 mL
¾ cup	chopped hazelnuts	175 mL
½ cup	flaked coconut	125 mL
¾ cup	grated apple	175 mL

Combine the flour with the maple syrup. Stir in the baking soda, cinnamon, salt and eggs, 1 at a time. Add the oil and maple cream liqueur. Mix well. Combine the remaining ingredients and stir into the flour mixture. Spray mini-loaf pans or large muffin tins with non-stick spray. Spoon batter into pans.

Temperature: 350°F (180°C)

Baking Time: 20 minutes

Yield: 24 mini-loaves or 30 muffins

Blueberry Maple Muffins

The abundance of blueberries in this recipe is very satisfying. These muffins will serve as a pick-me-up in the office when your blood sugar level is sagging.

½ cup	unsalted butter	125 mL
½ cup	maple sugar	125 mL
⅓ cup	maple syrup	75 mL
1 cup	whole milk	250 mL
2	eggs	2
2 cups	cake/pastry flour	500 mL
1 tbsp.	baking powder	15 mL
2 cups	fresh or frozen blueberries	500 mL

Blueberry Maple Muffins
(continued)

Cream butter and maple sugar together until the mixture is light and creamy. Stir in maple syrup. Add milk and then the eggs, 1 at a time. Mix well. Add cake flour and baking powder and mix again. Fold in blueberries.

Spray muffin cups with non-stick spray or line with muffin liners. Spoon or pour batter into muffin cups, filling two-thirds full. If you want more muffins, just double the recipe. It's best to eat muffins within 24 hours.

Temperature: 375°F (190°C)

Baking Time: 20 minutes

Yield: 12 muffins

Maple Mango Muffins

The increased consumption of mangoes in North America has resulted in some delicious combinations. Here's a recipe that makes a wonderful breakfast offering. Serve the mango muffins with marmalade and fresh strawberries.

2¼ cups	self-rising flour	550 mL
½ cup	maple sugar	125 mL
½ cup	chopped macadamia nuts	125 mL
⅔ cup	unsalted butter	150 mL
¼ cup	maple syrup	60 mL
2 cups	puréed mango pulp	500 mL
1 tbsp.	maple syrup liqueur	15 mL
⅔ cup	whole milk	150 mL
2	eggs, beaten	2

Place the flour, maple sugar and macadamia nuts in a bowl. Place the butter and maple syrup in a small saucepan and melt over low heat. Remove from heat. Purée the mangoes in a blender and add to the maple syrup/ butter mixture. In a separate bowl, mix the milk and eggs and add to the mango mixture. Add to the flour and incorporate completely.

Spray muffin cups with non-stick spray and pour in batter, filling cups two-thirds full.

Temperature: 375°F (190°C)

Baking Time: 20 minutes

Yield: 12 muffins

Cleary's Maple Chip Muffins

Cleary's Maple Products of Robertsonville, Quebec produces wonderful maple syrup and other maple items which are distributed all over the world. Jo-Ann Cleary provided this wonderful recipe for Maple Moon™ and it is another sensational breakfast offering.

1 cup	all-purpose flour	250 mL
½ cup	packed brown sugar	125 mL
½ cup	white sugar	125 mL
1½ tsp.	baking powder	7 mL
½ tsp.	salt	2 mL
1¾ cups	whole milk	425 mL
2	eggs, slightly beaten	2
½ cup	butter, melted and cooled	125 mL
1 tsp.	vanilla extract	5 mL
1½ cups	Cleary's Pure Maple Sugar Chunks	375 mL
½ cup	coarsely chopped pecans	125 mL

Place the flour, sugars, baking powder and salt in a large bowl. In a second bowl, mix milk, eggs, butter and vanilla until ingredients are completely incorporated. Make a well in the centre of the dry ingredients and stir in the milk mixture just to combine. Finally, stir in maple sugar chunks and nuts.

Grease and flour 12 muffin cups or spray them with non-stick spray. Pour the batter into the cups, filling them two-thirds full.

Temperature: 400°F (200°C)

Baking Time: 15 to 20 minutes

Allow the muffins to cool for 5 minutes before removing them from the pan.

Yield: 12 muffins

Maple Banana Bread

At our house there are always five or so black bananas sitting in the freezer, waiting for me to make them into banana bread. I can't possibly throw them out after the hardworking folks in Ecuador have harvested them and shipped them to Los Angeles for redistribution throughout North America. It's just too long a journey and too much human effort to end up in a landfill site. Besides, my mama's voice is always in my head – "You should do something with those bananas." Point taken.

1 cup	unsalted butter	250 mL
1⅓ cups	maple syrup	325 mL
3	large eggs, room temperature	3
2½ cups	overripe, mashed bananas	625 mL
2 cups	cake/pastry flour	500 mL
2 tsp.	baking powder	10 mL
1 tsp.	salt	5 mL
½ cup	Dutch OR Belgian chocolate chips	125 mL
½ cup	chopped hazelnuts	125 mL

In a large bowl, combine butter and maple syrup. Add eggs, 1 at a time, and beat well. Stir in bananas. Add flour, baking powder and salt. Mix completely and then add chocolate and hazelnuts. Pour into 2, 5 x 9" (12 x 23 cm), greased and floured loaf pans.

Temperature: 350°F (180°C)

Baking Time: 1 hour to 1 hour 15 minutes

Yield: 2 loaves

Maple Blueberry Bread

Blueberries are so good for you. This is a great way to get your day started. If you serve this with eggs and fruit, you have a lovely breakfast.

⅔ cup	soft, unsalted butter	150 mL
1⅓ cups	maple syrup	325 mL
3	eggs, at room temperature	3
⅔ cup	fresh buttermilk	150 mL
2 tbsp.	lemon zest	30 mL
2 cups	all-purpose flour	500 mL
2 tsp.	baking powder	10 mL
1 tsp.	salt	5 mL
2 cups	fresh or frozen blueberries	500 mL
3 tbsp.	flour (for frozen berries)	45 mL

Maple Lemon Glaze:

¼ cup	lemon juice	60 mL
½ cup	maple sugar	125 mL

Combine the butter and maple syrup well. Add the eggs, 1 at a time, and mix again. Add the buttermilk and lemon zest and mix again. In a separate bowl, combine the flour, baking powder and salt. Add to liquid batter and mix well. Do not over mix.

Place blueberries in a separate bowl. If they are frozen, add the 3 tbsp. (45 mL) of flour and toss. Fold the berries into the batter. Pour the batter into a greased and floured 5 x 9" (12 x 23 cm) loaf pan.

Temperature: 350°F (180°C)

Baking Time: 1¼ to 1½ hours*

To make the glaze, heat the lemon juice in a small saucepan. Dissolve the maple sugar in the hot lemon juice. When you remove the baked loaf from the oven, spoon the glaze over the top and allow to cool for about 30 minutes. Serve for breakfast.

Serves: 10

* *Check the bread at various times after 1 hour as "doneness" seems to vary with ovens and altitude.*

Pumpkin Maple Breakfast Bread

This is a great way to get started on cold mornings when you don't want to go out but you know you have to. Make this the night before and serve the next morning with scrambled eggs.

2 cups	sugar	500 mL
½ cup	maple syrup	125 mL
1 cup	canned pumpkin	250 mL
1½ cups	applesauce	375 mL
⅔ cup	vegetable oil	150 mL
3	eggs	3
½ cup	whole milk	125 mL
3½ cups	all-purpose flour	875 mL
1½ tsp.	baking powder	7 mL
1 tsp.	baking soda	5 mL
1 tbsp.	cinnamon	15 mL
1 tsp.	maple whiskey	5 mL
1 cup	chopped pecans	250 mL
1 cup	dark raisins	250 mL
½ cup	Dutch chocolate chips	125 mL

Place the sugar in a large mixing bowl. Add the next 6 ingredients and mix well on medium with an electric mixer. Sift the dry ingredients and add to the pumpkin mixture. Mix well and add the remaining ingredients. Mix again.

Pour the batter into 2 greased and floured 5 x 9" (3 x 23 cm) loaf pans.

Temperature: 350°F (180°C)

Baking Time: 1 hour, or until an inserted skewer or fork comes out clean

Yield: 2 loaves

Maple Coffee Cake

Rich and sweet, coffee cakes summon up images of farm breakfasts, morning coffee with good friends and substantial brunches. This version will satisfy everyone.

1 cup	raisins	250 mL
1 cup	coarsely chopped pecans	250 mL
1 tsp.	baking soda	5 mL
1 tsp.	baking powder	5 mL
1 cup	very strong coffee, boiling	250 mL
½ cup	unsalted butter	125 mL
¾ cup	maple syrup	175 mL
2	eggs	2
½ tsp.	salt	2 mL
2 tsp.	cinnamon	10 mL
1⅓ cups	cake/pastry flour	325 mL
1 tbsp.	lemon juice	15 mL

Combine the raisins and pecans in a large bowl. Sprinkle baking soda and baking powder over them and add boiling coffee. Set aside to cool.

In a separate bowl, mix butter and maple syrup. Add eggs, 1 at a time. Mix salt, cinnamon and flour and add this, alternately, with the raisin/pecan mixture, to the butter and maple syrup. Stir in lemon juice and pour batter into a greased and floured 8 x 12" (20 x 30 cm) cake pan.

Temperature: 350°F (180°C)

Baking Time: 45 minutes (test for doneness)

Serves: 10 to 12

Variation: To serve with **Maple Whipped Cream**, sweeten 2 cups (500 mL) of whipping cream with 3 to 5 tbsp. (45 to 75 mL) of maple syrup or maple sugar and beat until stiff. Serve Maple Coffee Cake with large dollops of whipped cream.

Maple
Soups,
Salads,
Vegetables
&
Sauces

The Maple Tree

"Many times I thought that if the particular tree . . . under which I was riding or walking was the only one like it in the country," wrote Henry David Thoreau, "it would be worth a journey across the continent to see it." (January 18, 1888)

Like Thoreau, poets and writers have been inspired through the ages by the essential divinity of the maple tree. Its soft, lime green essence in the spring yields to darker foliage in the height of summer, while the fall renders it so magnificent that admirers come from around the world to witness its collective beauty. The maple captures the soul in the fall but it is in the spring, the season of the maple moon, that the running of the sap captures the imagination.

The respect accorded to the sugar bush was entrenched in the norms of the Minnesota Ojibwa. Every adult female was granted her own sugar hut. This hut was claimed by right of descent through her mother's family and totem. The women of the tribe spent much time in their sugar huts collecting sap and creating the various maple products. Remarkably enough, the men of the tribe, who usually thought such tasks beneath them, would deviate from their usual pattern of hunting and fishing and actually assist in the harvesting of the sap.

It takes about forty gallons of maple sap to yield one gallon of maple syrup. The first run of sap is always the best and, historically, the most sought after because of its higher grade. "The first run, like first love, is always the best," John Burroughs wrote in *Winter Sunshine* in 1881, "always the fullest, always the sweetest; while there is a purity and delicacy of flavour about the sugar that far surpasses any subsequent yield." And as Dr. Benjamin Rush, signatory to the Declaration of Independence, wrote to Thomas Jefferson in 1792, "The gift of the sugar maple trees is from a benevolent Providence."

This miracle of life did not elude Thomas Jefferson. He loved the country and he loved maple trees. So enamoured was he of the sugar maple that he reportedly used no other type of sweetener. Over two hundred years later, this writer can see why Jefferson was so in awe of the great maple. In the spring, billions of trillions of cells will start to multiply all over the northern hemisphere as the sun and the soil gently ease our earth into spring. Trembling aspen, birch and maple gently offer up their lime green foliage. The brittle season of a million diamonds is suddenly gone. Cold nights and warm days push the sap slowly up into the trunk of the great trees. If an ice storm has hit during the winter, the sap haemorrhages from the broken branches and trunks and gushes forth with its sweet bounty. The sap icicles are an after-storm delight.

The Maple Tree

(continued)

The debt that we owe to trees is clearly huge. The life processes of trees make them, collectively, the "lungs of the earth". We live because of trees. The oldest tree in the world, ginkgo biloba, is used to enhance memory. It is unfortunate that we are so cavalier with the presence of trees. In recent years, clear cuts, acid rain, rapid urbanization and negligence have all taken their toll on the great forests of the earth. This is also very true of the rock or sugar maple.

The earth is home to over a hundred different types of maple trees. Some of them are softwoods, but it is the sap of the rock maple that produces the vast majority of what is ultimately termed "maple syrup". The production itself is not easy but it is generally true that nothing of value ever comes easily. As Canadians, we can be proud that, with a lot of hard work, our country produces two-thirds of the earth's maple syrup. It is no wonder that the maple leaf symbol plays such an important part in our daily lives.

Maple Cream of Carrot Soup

If the winter carrots that you use for your standard cream of carrot soup aren't sweet enough, the addition of a little maple syrup will make your family and guests think that you have used the first, sweet carrots of summer. Use vegetable stock if you are a practising or aspiring vegetarian.

4 cups	steamed sliced carrots	1 L
2	medium onions, steamed and quartered	2
2 cups	whole milk	500 mL
2 cups	chicken OR vegetable stock (see recipes on pages 37 and 38)	500 mL
½ cup	butter OR margarine	125 mL
½ cup	maple syrup	125 mL
1 cup	water	250 mL
4 tbsp.	flour	60 mL
1 cup	cream	250 mL
1 tsp.	Maggi Seasoning*	5 mL

Purée all of the ingredients in a food processor in batches. Purée to an even consistency. Transfer to a soup pot and bring to a very low boil. Simmer for about 30 to 35 minutes.

Serve with a crusty French baguette.

Serves: 6

* This is a flavouring that my mama always used. For years we have had a maggi plant growing in the garden. My mama dries it and throws it into all soups. The herb incorporates in a less "messy" fashion if you buy the extract from the plant. If you use it dried, it messes up the physical appearance of your recipe, although the flavour is wonderful. Maggi is available at all European delicatessens and large supermarkets.

Other names for maggi, more commonly known in North America, are lovage, sea parsley and smellage. Easy to grow, lovage looks and smells similar to celery but it can reach up to 6 to 10' (180 to 300 cm). It is sometimes used as a salt substitute in soups and stews, but the flavour is very strong, so use it sparingly. The ancient Greeks and Romans used lovage as a seasoning, in love potions and in medicines. They chewed the seed to aid digestion and relieve flatulence. The hollow stems can be used as straws and as a celery substitute in Caesars and Bloody Marys.

Creamy Maple Corn Soup

The title of this book is a tribute to the North American native tribes who used the maple tree's sap as a core part of their diet. Early members of the clergy, settlers, fur traders and explorers report that cultivated corn and tobacco were also central to the native lifestyle. This soup is a fusion between yesterday and today.

12	ears of fresh corn	12
½ cup	butter	125 mL
2	large yellow onions, chopped	2
½ cup	chopped green onions	125 mL
12 cups	vegetable stock (see recipe on page 37)	3 L
½ cup	maple syrup	125 mL
2 cups	cream	500 mL
1 tsp.	sea salt	5 mL
	freshly ground black pepper to taste	
	cilantro OR parsley for garnish	

Steam or boil the corn until completely tender (this is usually about 8 minutes under a full, rolling boil). Strip the corn from the cobs and set the corn aside.

Melt butter in a large saucepan. Add yellow and green onions and cook until translucent. Set aside.

Place the corn in a blender and purée. Add the onion mixture and purée until the consistency is smooth. Place the purée in a large soup pot and add the vegetable stock and maple syrup. Bring to a slow boil and simmer for about 25 minutes. Add the cream and sea salt. Cook over low to medium heat for another 5 minutes. Add black pepper to taste and garnish with cilantro or parsley. Serve immediately.

Serves: 8

Maple Mushroom Soup

My two best friends have switched to vegetarianism. It was probably time because entire herds of cows disappeared in the days when they were omnivorous. Here's a sublime vegetarian mushroom soup.

3 tbsp.	olive oil	45 mL
2 cups	chopped sweet, yellow onions	500 mL
3 tbsp.	minced garlic	45 mL
⅓ cup	maple syrup	75 mL
1-2	sweet red peppers, chopped	1-2
⅓ cup	chopped fresh parsley	75 mL
5 cups	sliced fresh Portobello OR oyster mushrooms	1.25 L
7 cups	vegetable stock (see recipe on page 37) freshly ground black pepper	1.75 L

Place olive oil in a large saucepan and add onions and garlic. Cook for 5 to 7 minutes over medium heat, until onions are soft and translucent.

Add the maple syrup, red peppers, parsley and mushrooms and cook for another 15 to 20 minutes. Stir frequently, until no liquid is left. Onions must be golden brown. Add the stock and bring to a boil. Simmer for approximately 15 minutes. Serve immediately with a crusty whole-grain baguette.

Serves: 6

Note: If you prefer a **Creamy Mushroom Soup**, purée the cooked vegetables and then add them to the vegetable stock prior to simmering.

Maple Gouda Soup

If you love Dutch cheese and soup the way my children do, this soup will become a tradition in your household. It takes about 1½ hours to make.

⅓ cup	unsalted butter	75 mL
4 cups	chopped leek, white parts only	1 L
2	medium yellow onions, chopped	2
1 tbsp.	minced garlic	15 mL
1½ cups	chopped Portobello mushrooms	375 mL
¼ cup	maple syrup	60 mL
4 cups	vegetable OR chicken stock (I prefer vegetable (see recipes on pages 37 and 38)	1 L
⅓ cup	all-purpose flour	75 mL
3 cups	water	750 mL
1 tsp.	sea salt	5 mL
1	whole baby Gouda cheese (10½ oz./ 300 g), diced	1
2 tbsp.	chopped fresh parsley	30 mL

In a large saucepan, melt the butter and sauté the leek, onions, garlic and mushrooms over medium heat for about 10 minutes. Remove from the heat and add the syrup and vegetable stock. Blend in the flour and water and return to the heat. Simmer, covered, for about 20 minutes Add the cheese for the last 5 minutes. Stir and heat until the cheese is melted.

Add the parsley just before serving. Serve immediately with a crusty baguette.

Serves: 8

Note: This soup can also be puréed. Just place the cooked vegetables in a blender and purée prior to simmering with the syrup/stock mixture.

Pictured on page 18.

Maple Brown Bean Soup

Beans – protein, calcium, iron and great flavour – you can't beat this hearty combination!

3 cups	dried brown beans	750 mL
2½ qts.	water	2.5 L
6 tbsp.	butter OR margarine	90 mL
6	leeks, washed, chopped (white parts only)	6
1	bunch leaf celery, chopped (do not use outside green leaves)	1
1 tsp.	salt	5 mL
½ tsp.	cayenne pepper	2 mL
1 tsp.	Maggi Seasoning*	5 mL
¼ cup	maple syrup	60 mL
3 tbsp.	sweet soy sauce	45 mL
1 cup	cubed ham	250 mL
	salt and pepper to taste	

In a large, heavy saucepan, soak the brown beans overnight, for at least 12 hours. Always start with cold water. The next morning, drain the beans and add fresh water; bring the beans to a boil and then simmer, covered, for about 3 hours. Test to see if they are done.

Melt the butter; add the leek and sauté for about 20 minutes. Add to the cooked beans along with the celery, spices, maple syrup, soy sauce and ham. Let the soup simmer for at least another 30 minutes. When finished, add salt and pepper to taste.

Serve with generous portions of thick, buttered pumpernickel or sour rye bread.

Serves: 6

* See the maggi note on page 32.

Vegetable Stock

Good stock is the basis for great soup – it's worth the effort. When you have time, try this and you'll agree.

1 cup	finely chopped onion	250 mL
3 tbsp.	vegetable oil	45 mL
3	leeks, chopped, white parts only	3
½ cup	winter carrots	125 mL
½ cup	rutabaga	125 mL
½ cup	parsnips	125 mL
½ cup	chopped celery (tender parts)	125 mL
1 cup	shredded lettuce	250 mL
½ tsp.	white pepper	2 mL
½ tsp.	black pepper	2 mL
1	bay leaf	1
½ tsp.	salt	2 mL
3	whole cloves	3
3 qts.	cold water	3 L
1 tsp.	Maggi Seasoning*	5 mL
2 sprigs	fresh thyme OR 1 tbsp. (15 mL) dried	2 sprigs
2 sprigs	fresh parsley OR 1 tbsp. (15 mL) dried	2 sprigs
1 tbsp.	marjoram	15 mL

Sauté the onions in the oil until very tender. Add all of the vegetables and spices, except the Maggi, thyme, parsley and marjoram, to the stock pot and cover with cold water. Bring the vegetables to a boil and then simmer over the lowest heat possible for about 2 hours. Add the remaining spices during the last half hour of cooking. Strain the stock and discard the vegetables.

Yield: 2 quarts (2 L)

* See the maggi note on page 32.

Chicken Stock

Low heat is the key to good clear chicken stock. It freezes well and is very flavourful.

6 lbs.	chicken backs, necks and wings	3 kg
6 qts.	cold water	6 L
½ tsp.	marjoram	2 mL
½ tsp.	thyme	2 mL
1 tsp.	fresh maggi OR Maggi Seasoning*	5 mL
1	bay leaf	1
1 tsp.	black pepper	5 mL
8	whole cloves	8
2	leeks, diced (white parts only)	2
½ cup	chopped parsley	125 mL
1	large yellow onion, chopped	1
1 cup	chopped celery, ribs only	250 mL
2	large winter carrots, chopped	2

Immerse the chicken pieces in cold water and bring to a boil. Let the chicken boil for about 5 minutes. Drain off the water and place the chicken in 6 quarts (6 L) of cold water. Bring the water to just a boil. Add the remaining ingredients.

From time to time you will need to remove the scum from the top of the water. Simmer for about 5 hours over very low heat. If you feel you need a little extra water in the pot, add 1 cup (250 mL) or so of warm water. Keep the stock covered throughout and make sure that you keep the heat low – DO NOT BOIL.

Strain the stock and discard the chicken and vegetables. Refrigerate the stock overnight.

Yields: 3 quarts (3 L)

* See the maggi note on page 32.

Maple Mango Spinach Salad

You can throw feta cheese into this salad to include enough protein in it so that you can call it a meal. It's great on hot summer days when you don't want to cook. Substitute chèvre for feta if you wish.

6 cups	fresh spinach, washed and torn into bite-sized pieces	1.5 L
6 cups	romaine hearts, washed and torn into bite-sized pieces	1.5 L
3	Belgian endive, cored and broken into leaves	3
2 cups	seedless red grapes	500 mL
1 cup	dark raisins	250 mL
1 cup	macadamia nuts, halved	250 mL
2	ripe avocados, peeled, pitted and cut into wedges	2
3 cups	sliced mango, fresh or canned, drained	750 mL

Maple Vinaigrette:

⅓ cup	extra virgin olive oil	75 mL
⅓ cup	vinegar*	75 mL
⅓ cup	maple syrup	75 mL
½ tsp.	salt	2 mL

Toss all salad ingredients together in a large salad bowl. Shake the dressing ingredients together and toss with the salad. Serve on chilled glass plates.

Serves: 8

    * *I use nasturtium vinegar or white wine vinegar. With balsamic vinegar, cut the quantity down to 3 tbsp. (45 mL) because of the intensity of the flavour.*

Note: If you want to use some of this salad for the following day, reserve dressing in a separate container and toss when needed.

Pictured on page 51.

Summer Evening Salad

When the days are long and hot and you don't want to eat a heavy meal, this is a great alternative to "cooking", especially if you have the dressing made ahead of time.

Maple Raspberry Vinaigrette:

½ cup	raspberry vinegar	125 mL
¼ cup	sunflower oil	60 mL
¼ cup	maple syrup	60 mL
1 tbsp.	strained lemon juice	15 mL
1	small butter lettuce, washed and torn into small pieces	1
1	heart of romaine, washed and chopped	1
2 cups	chopped fresh spinach	500 mL
1 cup	pineapple tidbits, drained	250 mL
1 cup	cantaloupe balls	250 mL
1 cup	fresh blueberries	250 mL
1 cup	fresh strawberries	250 mL
1 cup	green grapes	250 mL
1 cup	chopped fresh mango	250 mL
½ cup	Black Forest ham, cut into small pieces	125 mL
1 cup	cubed baby Gouda cheese	250 mL

Mix all of the dressing ingredients in a small bowl and place in the refrigerator for about 1 hour.

Gently toss all of the salad ingredients, saving the ham and cheese for the top. Pour the salad dressing over the salad. Toss and serve.

Serves: 6

Note: If you prefer very little dressing, use less and reserve the excess for future use.

 aple Fatoosh

Fatoosh is a popular Middle Eastern bread salad that is made with toasted crisp pita bread – their answer to croûtons. Central to the Middle Eastern diet is the use of honey as a sweetener. I thought that this would be a nice way to mix Middle Eastern preferences with two distinctly North American products. I just add what I like, and what the kids like.

1	head of romaine lettuce, outside coarse leaves removed and insides chopped	1
1	long English cucumber, peeled and sliced	1
1	red pepper, seeded and chopped	1
1	yellow pepper, seeded and chopped	1
1	orange pepper, seeded and chopped	1
2 cups	seedless green grapes	500 mL
½ cup	chopped parsley	125 mL
½ cup	chopped green onions	125 mL
2 cups	halved cherry tomatoes	500 mL
2 cups	crumbled feta cheese	500 mL
30	large tortilla chips, broken up*	30

Maple Cilantro Dressing:

¼ cup	lemon juice	60 mL
¼ cup	extra virgin olive oil	60 mL
½ cup	chopped fresh cilantro	125 mL
⅓ cup	maple syrup	75 mL
1 tsp.	sea salt	5 mL
	dried red pepper flakes (optional)	

Mix all of the salad ingredients in a very large salad bowl. Mix the dressing in a separate bowl and pour over the salad. Toss and serve. Use the dressing according to your judgment, some people like more dressing, some like less.

Serves: 8

* This is a good salad for getting rid of those annoying bottom-of-the-bag chips that the kids won't eat because they are fussy and the chips aren't perfect.

August Garden Salad

In most parts of Canada, and certain parts of the United States, August is the month when vegetables pour onto the markets. If you have a garden you are faced with the old "feast or famine" syndrome. This salad addresses the concern of "what to do with all those vegetables", at least temporarily. If all of the ingredients come fresh from the garden, and you serve it for two days, it's a nice "diet" salad as well.

Balsamic Maple Dressing:

1¼ cups	maple syrup	300 mL
1 cup	vinegar	250 mL
2 tbsp.	balsamic vinegar	30 mL
¾ cup	sunflower oil	175 mL
1½ tbsp.	mustard powder	22 mL
1 tbsp.	celery seed	15 mL
1 tsp.	sea salt	5 mL
½ cup	chopped red pepper	125 mL
½ cup	chopped yellow pepper	125 mL
½ cup	broccoli florets	125 mL
1 cup	thinly sliced carrots	250 mL
½ cup	chopped yellow onion	125 mL
1	small head of red cabbage, finely shredded, all large spines removed	1
½ cup	quartered mushrooms	125 mL
1 cup	chopped cucumber	250 mL
¼ cup	finely chopped parsley	60 mL

Combine all of the dressing ingredients in a medium saucepan and bring to a boil. Boil for 1 to 2 minutes; remove from the heat and cool in the refrigerator for about an hour.

Place a steaming basket in a very large pot and add water. Steam the peppers, broccoli, carrots, onion and red cabbage for 3 to 4 minutes. Remove from the heat and cool. Place the steamed vegetables and the mushrooms, cucumber and parsley in a large glass salad bowl. Toss the vegetables with as much of the cooled dressing as you like.

Serves: 8

aple Coleslaw

Coleslaw is the kind of recipe that can be great or brutal. Although North America has the safest food supply in the world, in many restaurants coleslaw comes dyed in obscure colours, looking as though it has been stored since the First Great War. There should be a law that after two to three days coleslaw should no longer be recycled. This recipe is standard, nutritious fare with a maple twist.

Maple Mustard Dressing:

½ cup	sunflower oil	125 mL
½ cup	vinegar	125 mL
¼ cup	maple syrup	60 mL
1 tsp.	mustard powder	5 mL
1 tsp.	salt	5 mL
½ tsp.	pepper	2 mL
1 tbsp.	celery seeds	15 mL
½	large head of cabbage, finely shredded	½
1	small red onion, sliced into thin rings	1
1	yellow onion, sliced into thin rings	1
3	carrots, grated	3
1	red pepper, finely chopped	1
¼ cup	finely chopped parsley	60 mL

Place all of the dressing ingredients in a 5-cup (1.25 L) saucepan. Bring to a boil and then simmer for about 2 minutes. Remove from the heat and cool. Refrigerate for 2 to 3 hours.

Place all of the vegetables in a large glass salad bowl and pour the cooled dressing over the vegetables. Toss and serve immediately.

Serves: 6 to 8

Lobster and Avocado Salad
with Maple Dressing

The maple syrup in this dressing makes "fishy stuff" a soft sell for children.

4 cups	lobster meat	1 L
4	soft avocados, peeled and cut into wedges	4
½ cup	chopped cilantro	125 mL
1 cup	red raspberries	250 mL

Nasturtium Maple Dressing:

¼ cup	extra virgin olive oil OR sunflower oil	60 mL
¼ cup	nasturtium OR red raspberry vinegar	60 mL
¼ cup	maple syrup	60 mL
	freshly ground black pepper	

If you can find fresh, cooked lobster, buy it and use it. Otherwise, you are going to have to go the distance, buy the live lobsters and cook them in salted boiling water until they turn bright red. Shell when cooled and measure out the required amount.

Combine lobster, avocado, cilantro and raspberries.

Combine all dressing ingredients in a bottle; shake well. Toss the salad with the dressing. Use only what you need and reserve the remaining dressing.

Serves: 4 to 6, depending on appetites

Variation: If fresh crab meat is your favourite, or more accessible, substitute crab meat for lobster in this recipe.

Turkey Hill Red Cabbage

Turkey Hill Sugarbush Ltd. kindly provided this recipe. They have developed recipes to accompany the myriad of excellent syrup products that they distribute all over the world.

1	medium-sized red cabbage	1
1½ tsp.	salt	7 mL
¼ tsp.	pepper	1 mL
⅛ tsp.	grated nutmeg	0.5 mL
3 tbsp.	vinegar	45 mL
2	large cooking apples	2
3 tbsp.	pure maple syrup	45 mL

Quarter and core the washed cabbage and cut into fine strips. Season with salt, pepper, nutmeg and vinegar and mix thoroughly. Place the cabbage in a well-buttered casserole; cover and bake.

Temperature: 350°F (180°C)

Baking Time: 45 minutes

Peel, core and slice the apples. Stir apples and maple syrup into the cabbage and cook, covered, for another 30 minutes. Serve in the casserole.

Serves: 6

Molly's Maple Carrots

Our golden retriever, Molly, is on a diet. The veterinarian advised giving her raw carrots but all she does is just look at them. She prefers them this way.

8-10	large carrots, sliced	8-10
¼ cup	butter	60 mL
½ cup	maple syrup	125 mL
4 tbsp.	chopped chives OR parsley	60 mL
	salt and pepper to taste	

Steam the carrots until they are tender. Place all of the remaining ingredients in a saucepan and stir well. Pour the warm maple butter over the carrots and serve warm.

Serves: 4

Maple Carrots, Leek & Cauliflower

As a child, I wouldn't eat cauliflower unless my mama made a white sauce to go with it and put paprika on top. Maple syrup was difficult to come by, but I would have eaten more vegetables if she'd made them this way.

6 cups	baby carrots (preferably from the garden)	1.5 L
4	leeks (white parts only)	4
4 cups	small cauliflower florets	1 L
4 cups	water	1 L

Maple Cinnamon Sauce:

½ cup	butter	125 mL
1 cup	maple syrup	250 mL
1 tsp.	cinnamon (optional)	5 mL

Place vegetables in a steamer or a pot with a steaming basket. Steam, covered, until tender. Set aside.

To make the sauce, melt butter in a skillet and add maple syrup and cinnamon. Pour over vegetables according to taste and serve immediately. Reserve any leftover sauce for the next time.

Serves: 6 to 8

Pictured on page 87.

Maple Winter Vegetables

Children love vegetables if you sweeten them up a little. This is especially true of vegetables that have been stored in warehouses since the harvest. If you tell them the magical story of the way the maple tree sucks the sweetness of the earth into its trunk just for them, vegetables are an easy sell.

4	leeks (white parts only)	4
1½ cups	butternut squash, chunked	375 mL
3	parsnips, cut up	3
2	onions	2
5	carrots	5
4 tbsp.	unsalted butter	60 mL
¼ cup	maple syrup	60 mL
1 tsp.	salt	5 mL
1 tsp.	pepper	5 mL
	fresh parsley, dill OR cilantro	

Maple Winter Vegetables
(continued)

Clean the leeks and slice crosswise. Chunk butternut squash. Peel parsnips and slice into coin-sized pieces. Peel the onions and cut into thin wedges. Peel carrots and cut into coin-sized pieces. Place all of the vegetables in a steamer or use a steamer basket placed in a large pot. Cover and steam until all of the vegetables are tender.

In a saucepan, melt the butter with the maple syrup. Pour over the steamed vegetables and add salt and pepper to taste. Sprinkle with your choice of fresh herbs.

Serves: 6 to 8

Pictured on page 69.

Baked Maple Squash

When I was a child, we had an outhouse for a while. As immigrants, we were what I now refer to as nouveau pauvre. Mamu would make us eat spinach because she wanted us to be healthy. I'd wad up a bunch in the corner of my mouth, go outside and head to the outhouse where it was strategically expectorated down the hole. Now I like vegetables so much that I feel they are the best part of the meal. This is particularly true of squash. It is divine with maple syrup.

5 cups	steamed butternut, acorn OR spaghetti squash	1.25 L
3	egg whites, lightly beaten	3
⅓ cup	maple syrup	75 mL
4 tbsp.	butter	60 mL
1½ tsp.	cinnamon	7 mL
1 cup	slivered almonds	250 mL

Steam the squash in advance in a steamer or wrap in aluminum foil and bake in a hot oven until it is completely soft. Remove the squash from the oven and peel off the skin. Cool and mash the squash until it is the consistency of mashed potatoes.

Mix squash, egg whites, maple syrup, butter, cinnamon and almonds together. Grease an 8" (20 cm) square baking pan and spoon the squash into the pan.

Temperature: 400°F (200°C)

Baking Time: 20 to 25 minutes

Serves: 6

Maple Turnip Purée with Bacon

Surprise! Here's a good source of Vitamin C. Turnips are great with bacon and nutmeg – maple syrup adds the crowning touch.

2	large turnips cut into chunks	2
1 tsp.	salt	5 mL
1 tsp.	freshly ground black pepper	5 mL
½ cup	butter	125 mL
½ cup	maple syrup	125 mL
⅓ cup	heavy cream	75 mL
10 slices	lean bacon	10 slices
½ tsp.	freshly grated nutmeg	2 mL
5	sprigs fresh dill OR parsley for garnish	5

Steam the turnip chunks until tender and then sprinkle them with salt. Mash the turnips or purée them in a blender, mixer or food processor. Add the pepper and process once again.

Melt the butter in a saucepan and add the maple syrup. Mix thoroughly and stir into the turnips until all ingredients are thoroughly mixed. Stir in the cream.

Fry the bacon in a skillet until crisp. Drain off the bacon fat, reserving about 1 tbsp. (15 mL). Stir the nutmeg, bacon and reserved fat into the turnip mixture.

Garnish with the fresh green herbs and serve.

Serves: 6

Variation: This recipe is also adaptable to sweet potatoes and produces the same delicious results. Just substitute 2 medium-sized sweet potatoes for the turnips and use the remaining ingredients as is.

 48

Maple Baked Beans

This recipe is such a North American favourite that it seems almost sacrilegious to omit it. Molasses is traditional in this recipe, however, our family does not use molasses in anything because we feel that maple syrup is so much better. It is traditional to use salt pork in Quebec and Newfoundland, but most of us don't have a little piggy waltzing around on the Far Forty anymore. As a result, this recipe substitutes Canadian lean back bacon, which is more readily available.

4 cups	navy beans	1 L
1¼ cups	maple syrup	300 mL
2	onions, finely chopped	2
¾ lb.	Canadian back bacon, chopped	340 g
2 tsp.	dry mustard	10 mL
½ cup	ketchup	125 mL

Pick over the beans and soak them overnight in a quart (L) or so of hot water.

Drain the beans and place them in a large saucepan. Add water to the top of the beans and cover. Bring to a boil and then reduce heat to low. Simmer on low for about 1½ hours. Drain off the liquid and place the beans in a 3-quart (3 L) casserole.

Mix all of the remaining ingredients and add to the beans. Add enough fresh water to cover the beans.

Slow-cook the beans, covered, for 5 to 6 hours at 250°F (120°C). Check occasionally and add water as needed to keep the beans moist.

Bake the beans uncovered for the last hour.

Temperature: 250°F (120°C)

Baking Time: 5 to 6 hours

Serves: 6

Variation: Add ¼ cup (60 mL) Canadian Maple Whisky during the last 2 hours of cooking.

Oven-Roasted Maple Onion Potatoes

In China, caramelized potatoes, like caramelized apples, are a delicacy. These maple-glazed roasted potatoes are a more robust and equally delicious treat.

2 lbs.	potatoes, peeled and sliced	1 kg
2	large yellow onions, peeled and chopped	2
4 tbsp.	olive oil	60 mL
4 tbsp.	butter, melted	60 mL
½ cup	maple syrup	125 mL
1 tbsp.	minced garlic	15 mL
1 tsp.	salt	5 mL
1 tsp.	freshly ground black pepper	5 mL
1½ cups	chopped red pepper	375 mL
¾ cup	finely chopped mixed herbs: chives, parsley, dill and sage	175 mL

Use a large shallow baking dish. Spray the bottom and sides with non-stick spray and combine the potatoes and onions in the dish.

Combine oil, melted butter, maple syrup, garlic, salt and pepper and pour over potatoes and onions.

Bake, uncovered, on the middle rack of the oven. Bake for 30 minutes and then add the red pepper and fresh herbs. Mix well with the hot potatoes and onions and continue baking for another 15 to 20 minutes. Serve immediately.

Temperature: 450°F (230°C)

Baking Time: 30 minutes, then 15 to 20 minutes

Serves: 6

Pictured on page 87.

Maple Mango Spinach Salad, page 39

Maple Scalloped Potatoes

You can make this a vegetarian dish or you can add the ham but, either way, it's homey and my children love it. It may seem "high in fat", possibly the most hated three words in the English language. But, consider how often your children eat French Fries and this will seem a better choice.

12	medium potatoes, thinly sliced	12
½ cup	all-purpose flour	125 mL
	salt and pepper to taste	
1½ cups	cooked ham	375 mL
1½ cups	shredded mild Cheddar cheese	375 mL
½ cup	maple syrup	125 mL
1½ cups	thinly sliced onion	375 mL
1 tbsp.	minced garlic	15 mL
¼ cup	finely chopped parsley	60 mL
¼ cup	butter	60 mL
2¼ cups	half and half cream	550 mL

Grease or spray a 6-quart (6 L) ovenproof casserole with non-stick spray.

Place sliced potatoes in a large bowl and sprinkle with flour, salt and pepper. Mix well.

Layer the potatoes, ham, Cheddar cheese, maple syrup and onions in alternating layers until you have exhausted these ingredients. As you layer, sprinkle each layer with garlic and parsley.

Melt the butter and mix with half and half cream. You can try skim milk here if you are on a diet but it basically wrecks the recipe.

Pour the cream over the potato layers and place in a preheated oven. Bake, covered, for the first 30 minutes. Then uncover and bake uncovered for the last hour. Allow to stand for 30 minutes before serving. This is almost better the second day.

Temperature: 350°F (180°C)

Baking Time: 1½ hours

Serves: 8 to 10

Mango Maple Tiger Shrimp, page 64

Allison Duthie's Maple Rice Experience

Allison Duthie is 18 years of age. This is her favourite snack, so there goes the notion that all teens eat only junk food. This meal obviously adds to her intelligence because she demonstrates no lack of that.

2 cups	brown rice	500 mL
4-5 cups	water	1-1.25 L
1 tsp.	sea salt	5 mL

Bring the rice, water and salt to a boil. Lower the heat to simmer; cover and cook until done (about 45 minutes).

The following is Allison's prescription for health – given verbatim:

	rice (short-grain brown OR jasmine, depending on your mood)	
	almonds OR any other favourite nut (optional)	
smidge	**butter (optional)**	**smidge**
	100% pure maple syrup	

Make as much rice as you want (are you hungry or just feeling peckish?). You want the rice to be as perfect as possible (a rice cooker is an asset here).

Choose your favourite bowl, one that you can hold in your hand while you savour the maple syrupy goodness. Fill the bowl with as much rice as you can eat. Seconds and possibly thirds are definitely allowed !!

Optional butter step. For the ultimate comfort food, add a bit of butter to the steaming rice.

Drizzzzzzzzle the maple syrup over the rice. If you're a true maple freak, you'll pour on just enough so that a small pool forms beneath the steaming pile of rice. It'll be there after the rice is gone. (Please refer to "tip" for instructions on how to eat that little pool.)

Optional almonds or favourite nut step. Chopping is optional. If you're lazy, or just plain hankering for your tasty dish, throw them in whole. Nobody has to know.

Savour every bite! This dish is doubly good when being consumed while reading.

Decide whether or not you're hungry for more.

Tip: When you eat your rice and maple syrup, make sure that there's both a fork and a spoon available. The fork is used for eating the rice. The spoon is used to scrape every last drop of maple syrup off the bowl. If the bowl is small and shallow enough, lick it clean!

 54

Canadian Maple Wild Rice

Just think. In the marshes of Saskatchewan, Manitoba and Ontario, wild rice grows and is distributed to gourmet restaurants around the world. Those same marshes are also home to the magnificent loon, whose distinctive call is as much a signature to the Canadian identity as maple syrup. It makes sense that wild rice and maple syrup belong together. I substitute maple syrup for some of the water when steaming the rice. The nutty flavour is retained and it makes a great side dish. If you are a vegetarian, serve the wild rice with cheese and vegetables and you have a nutritious meal. Don't forget dessert.

2 cups	Canadian wild rice	500 mL
½ cup	maple syrup	125 mL
½ tsp.	salt	2 mL
6 cups	water	1.5 L
4 tbsp.	unsalted butter	60 mL

Place the wild rice in a saucepan with maple syrup, salt and water. Bring to a boil on high, then cover and reduce heat. Simmer for 45 minutes. When all of the water is boiled off, test the rice for tenderness and that distinctive nutty flavour. Stir the butter into the hot rice and serve.

Serves: 6 to 8

Maple Whisky Sauce

This is delicious with baked ham.

1 cup	Dijon mustard	250 mL
⅔ cup	maple syrup	175 mL
2 tbsp.	maple whisky	30 mL

In a small bowl, stir together mustard, syrup and maple whisky until they are well mixed.

Yield: about 1¾ cups (425 mL)

Saskatoon Berry Sauce

Add this to meat or fish dishes and your mama won't have to pull your eyelids down to check your iron levels. This beats liver any day.

4 cups	fresh or frozen saskatoon berries	1 L
1 cup	maple syrup	250 mL
½ cup	maple cream liqueur	125 mL
2	cinnamon sticks	2
⅓ cup	butter	75 mL

Combine all of the ingredients and bring to a boil in a medium saucepan. Do this very, very slowly as maple syrup tends to caramelize. Cover and cook for about 20 minutes, until the sauce has thickened. Serve this sauce over fish, beef or just as it is.

Yield: about 3½ cups (800 mL)

Thanksgiving Cranberries

My son Matthew's favourite holiday is Thanksgiving. I can understand why. It is not generally understood or discussed that the early settlers in both the United States and Canada faced the very real possibility of starvation if they weren't resourceful. They learned how to prepare and preserve indigenous fruits, vegetables and game, and they shared the bounty of a successful harvest in their new land. At our house, you can't have Thanksgiving without fresh cranberries.

3 cups	cranberries	750 mL
1 cup	maple syrup	250 mL
¾ cup	orange juice	175 mL

Combine all ingredients in a saucepan. Bring the mixture to a boil for only 1 to 2 minutes. Reduce heat and simmer, uncovered, until the sauce has set.

Be careful that you do NOT cook on high. Maple syrup caramelizes more quickly than sugar and the cranberries will be an unattractive, dark colour.

Yield: about 2 cups (500 mL)

Tropical Maple Syrup Glaze

This recipe combines the beauty of at least three trees: mango, lemon and maple. Combine that with the root crops, onion, garlic and ginger and you have an astoundingly flavourful glaze that you can use with ham, chicken or other poultry. If you are a vegetarian, use this sauce on wild rice, various vegetables, or just eat it right out of the jar. Anything is possible.

½ cup	butter	125 mL
½ cup	finely chopped onion	125 mL
1 tbsp.	minced garlic	15 mL
2 cups	maple syrup	500 mL
1 cup	chopped fresh mango	250 mL
¼ cup	chopped crystallized ginger	60 mL
½ cup	white vinegar	125 mL
¼ cup	maple sugar	60 mL
½ cup	fresh lemon juice, strained	125 mL
1 tbsp.	grated lemon zest	15 mL

Melt the butter in a saucepan. Use medium heat to avoid scorching. Heat until the butter bubbles and then add the onions and garlic. Cook the onions until they are translucent. Add the maple syrup, mango, ginger, vinegar, maple sugar, lemon juice and lemon zest. Cook for about 15 minutes over medium-low heat.

You can make this sauce ahead and refrigerate it for a few days. It's great when you have invited guests on one of those killer days when there are too many things to do and you still want to have an impressive meal.

Yield: about 4 cups (1 L)

Saskatoon Maple Barbecue Glaze

These berries are the fabulous fruit that grow on the Canadian prairies in high, gravelled areas. The natives pounded them into buffalo meat and made a super nutritious jerky called pemmican. Sort of the fast food of the eighteenth and nineteenth centuries. These berries are loaded with iron. When Saskatoon Pie was served at Vancouver's World Fair, Expo '86, people lined up for four to five blocks at the Saskatchewan Pavilion. You have to believe that there is some kind of magic going on when people wait that long for a piece of pie. If you are one of those unlucky folks that live in a place where you can't get saskatoons, substitute those lovely little blueberries that grow on the East Coast or the REALLY BIG ones that grow on the West Coast.

⅓ cup	butter	75 mL
2 tbsp.	minced garlic	30 mL
1 cup	finely chopped onion	250 mL
1 cup	saskatoon jam	250 mL
½ cup	white vinegar	125 mL
¼ cup	Worcestershire sauce	60 mL
1 cup	maple syrup	250 mL
1½ tsp.	fresh thyme	7 mL
1 tsp.	hot pepper sauce (optional)	5 mL
1½ cups	fresh or frozen saskatoons, for garnish	375 mL

Heat the butter over medium heat until it begins to bubble. Add garlic and onions. Cook until the onions are translucent. Add the saskatoon jam, vinegar, Worcestershire sauce, maple syrup, thyme and pepper sauce. Simmer for about 35 minutes, stirring more or less constantly.

Serve immediately or keep refrigerated for a maximum of 5 to 7 days in a covered container. Serve with meats, fish, ribs, sausages or on vegetables. When serving, sprinkle the fresh saskatoons over the entire dish for a beautiful presentation and good nutrition.

Yield: about 3½ cups (800 mL)

Maple
Main
Course
Dishes

Honouring The Maple Tree

Today's practice of clear-cutting forests, and the resulting outcry of environmentalists, has a collective predecessor in the history of maple syrup. So destructive were the collection practices of some of the settlers that, in 1872, Leander Coburn lamented in Vermont's first "Agricultural Report" that:

> There were many trees badly injured, and some were hollow from the effects of one year's tapping with an ax. The man that commenced on, and cleared up the farm used to tap with an ax; he would cut some 4 or 5 . . . gashes, one above the other, and then strike in his ax below these gashes and put in a spout as wide as the bit of his ax. The consequence was that in three or four years his sugar trees would be gone, and then he would move his boiling works to another place and commence with another stock of trees.

The fact that the rock maple can live for two to four hundred years, and cannot be tapped until it is about forty years of age, makes this a massive abuse of the gift of Providence. Bob Jakeman, of The Maple Store, in Ontario, is an expert on maple trees. He considers the productive life of a maple tree to be seventy to a hundred years – after it is forty to fifty years of age and ten inches in diameter. Bob's side road, Trillium Line, is lined with huge spreading maples on each side. They were planted around 1880 and they will live out their maturity.

There are two instances in Ontario where sugar maples have lived for over four hundred years. One was in Waterloo County, in a bush owned by Henry Merlau near Wellesley. This magnificent giant was toppled by wind in the 1980s. The other tree is in Lanark Country near Ottawa, Ontario. It is owned by George Drummond and is nicknamed "The Drummond Giant". This is said to be the oldest maple still alive in Canada.

Here in Canada, the Jakeman family keep their trees and honour them. They settled in Oxford County near Woodstock, Ontario, Canada in 1876, long before freeways, cars, airplanes and technology came to stay. They began making maple syrup for their household during that first year. Today, with prudent management, the Jakeman family are maple sugaring in the same forests where their ancestors sugared when they first arrived.

H*onouring The Maple Tree*
(continued)

Bob Jakeman says, "We are located just off Highway 401, at exit 230. We are easy to find." They are open six days a week during the off-season and seven days a week during the high season. Bob says,"Visitors are always welcome, and we ship worldwide from The Maple Store." Today, with the miracle of technology, anyone can order from The Maple Store at the touch of a finger.

Acid rain, urbanization and imprudent harvesting techniques have contributed to the demise of the maple. Yet, it often seems miraculous how nature can repair herself and yield gifts out of tragedy. Scientists are still amazed at how nature is rectifying the massive distortions created by the Mount St. Helen's blast in May 1980. So, too, with ice storms, witness the large icicles hanging from the broken branches of the rock or sugar maple. These icicles contain maple sap and are a delight to everyone who tastes them.

It is quite clear that environmentalists have made their mark with respect to the need to establish large nature preserves across North America. In Quebec and Ontario, Canada, as well as throughout New England, the rock or sugar maple requires vigilant protection to preserve it against the onslaught of "civilization". In Canada, our national symbol and the pride inherent in that symbol are at stake.

Maple Cheese Casserole

If you serve this with a salad, you have a lovely vegetarian meal. My youngest son, Allan, says he likes this fine but he likes "the potato stuff" better.

4 cups	cooked jasmine rice	1 L
6 cups	shredded mild Cheddar cheese	1.5 L
1	red pepper, chopped	1
1	yellow pepper, chopped	1
1	orange pepper, chopped	1
2 cups	chopped mushrooms	500 mL
5	eggs, well beaten	5
½ cup	maple syrup	125 mL
1½ cups	whole milk	375 mL
2 tsp.	sea salt	10 mL
1 cup	coarse bread crumbs	250 mL
½ cup	melted butter	125 mL

Spray a 9 x 13" (23 x 33 cm) baking pan with non-stick spray. Place a layer of rice and a layer of vegetables in the baking pan. Sprinkle the vegetables with Cheddar and then repeat the layer. Beat the eggs and mix in the maple syrup and milk. Add the salt and pour over the layers of rice, vegetables and cheese. Sprinkle with bread crumbs and drizzle with melted butter.

Temperature: 350°F (180°C)

Baking Time: 50 minutes

Serves: 8

Maple Crab Newburg

I know that a typical Newburg is made with sherry, but I can cheat because it's my book and my passion.

4 tbsp.	butter	60 mL
2 lbs.	Alaska king crab meat	1 kg
2 cups	cream	500 mL
3	egg yolks	3
⅓ cup	maple cream liqueur OR maple liqueur	75 mL
4 tbsp.	maple whisky*	60 mL
	salt and pepper to taste	
	harvest bread** toasted and cut into points	
	fresh dill sprigs	

Maple Crab Newburg
(continued)

Melt butter in a large skillet. Add crab meat and warm gently. Gradually add the cream and continue cooking over low heat. In a separate bowl, beat the egg yolks with the maple cream liqueur and whisky. Mix well and then add to the crab. Continue heating but DO NOT boil. Add salt and pepper to taste.

Serve on toast points and garnish with dill sprigs.

Serves 6

* *If you prefer, substitute maple syrup for the maple whisky. The flavour will be different but still mouth watering.*
** *Harvest bread is a multigrain crusty loaf with great texture and flavour.*

Maple Cream and Mushroom Scallops

East Coast bay scallops are small and sweet and at their peak in the fall. Sea scallops are best over the winter months. Succulent and sweet, scallops are perfect partners for the divine nectar of the maple.

18	crêpes (see Johnny's Skinny Pancakes on page 15)	18
½ cup	maple cream whisky	125 mL
1½ cups	chopped shiitake mushrooms	375 mL
3 cups	uncooked scallops	750 mL
⅓ cup	butter	75 mL
⅓ cup	flour	75 mL
2 cups	cream	500 mL
⅓ cup	chopped fresh dillweed	75 mL
¾ cup	grated Dutch Gouda Cheese	175 mL

Prepare the crêpes and set aside. Keep warm.

Use a large skillet and combine the maple whisky and mushrooms. Cover and simmer for 5 minutes. Add scallops for the last 2 to 3 minutes.

In a separate skillet, melt the butter. Add flour and stir constantly over medium heat. Add the cream and continue stirring. Do not boil. Add dillweed and then the scallop mixture. Roll the scallops and sauce in warmed crêpes and serve.

Serves: 4

Mango Maple Tiger Shrimp

Spicy salsa and rich, smooth maple syrup are a super combination in this exotic mango and shrimp dish.

¼ cup	butter	60 mL
1 cup	finely chopped onion	250 mL
1 tbsp.	minced garlic	15 mL
½ cup	ketchup	125 mL
1 cup	fruit salsa	250 mL
½ tsp.	chili powder	2 mL
1 tsp.	cinnamon	5 mL
¼ cup	lemon juice, strained	60 mL
½ cup	vinegar	125 mL
⅔ cup	maple syrup	150 mL
⅓ cup	soy sauce	75 mL
4 lbs.	fresh tiger shrimp	2 kg
1 cup	sliced mango	250 mL
1 cup	orange segments	250 mL
1 tsp.	salt	5 mL
1 tsp.	pepper	5 mL

Heat the butter over medium heat until it starts to bubble. Add onions and garlic and simmer over low to medium heat until the onions are translucent. Add ketchup, fruit salsa, chili powder, cinnamon, lemon juice, vinegar, maple syrup and soy sauce. Cook the sauce over low to medium heat for about 25 minutes, stirring frequently. Set aside, covered.

Meanwhile, steam shelled and deveined tiger shrimp, with tails attached, for 5 to 6 minutes, or until they are opaque.

Add tiger shrimp to maple sauce and add mango slices, orange sections, salt and pepper. Serve over a bed of rice or angel hair pasta.

Serves: 6

Pictured on page 52.

Dilled Arctic Char

with Saskatoon Berry Sauce

The late Father Raymond de Coccola left Sicily and lived among the Inuit in the thirties and forties. He lived in the igloos and would watch in amazement as the Inuit hunted elk in the summer and ate the fresh, partly digested grass of summer right out of the slaughtered elk's stomach. They loved these "greens" and considered them an incredible delicacy. Father Raymond preferred the Arctic char. Long after he had left the high Arctic, he yearned for this delicate white fish. For this recipe, you can use maple or cedar planks to cook on. Simply soak them before placing them in your barbecue. Place the char on top of the planks. This takes no time at all.

2	large bunches of fresh dill, chopped (reserve hard stems of dill bunches)	2
1 tbsp.	salt	15 mL
	freshly ground black pepper	
½ cup	maple whisky	125 mL
2	oranges, thinly sliced	2
½ cup	butter	125 mL
6	Arctic char, about 1 lb. (500 g) each	6

Combine all ingredients, except the char. Place soaked maple plank(s) on the barbecue grill. Close the lid and heat the planks for about 5 minutes. Divide the maple dill mixture among the 6 char, placing it inside and along the cavity of each fish. Lay the dill stems on top of the hot planks and place the fish on top of the dill stems. Close the barbecue lid and cook for 12 to 15 minutes, until the fish is opaque and the flesh flakes when a fork is inserted.

Serve with Saskatoon Berry Sauce, page 56, and Canadian Maple Wild Rice, page 55.

Serves: 6

Barbecued Salmon

This recipe, given to me by a friend, is a wonderful way to barbecue salmon over a wood fire. The coals add a fabulous smoky note to the rich salmon flavour.

- First you need to build a good fire. You should use either alder or birch. Birch is usually best. You need a good bed of coals over which to cook the salmon.

- After you have a good bed of coals you can prepare the salmon for cooking. The easiest way is to use two oven racks and put the salmon between them. You can use wire to fasten the racks together. The salmon should be filleted for best results. The fillets will cook faster and more evenly than the whole fish.

- The racks of salmon should be placed or propped up around the fire approximately a foot to two feet (30 to 60 cm) away from the fire, depending on the heat. It's important to keep a close eye on the salmon as it's cooking to make sure it doesn't get overcooked and dried out. To ensure even cooking throughout, the salmon needs to be turned. Rotate and turn the racks on a regular basis to keep the juices inside the salmon. I usually start with the salmon skin faced to the fire. Use a couple of pairs of pliers to accomplish this task.

- If you have a good fire the salmon should be done in about twenty minutes. You can tell by looking at it – it should have a white coating. The salmon fat should be oozing out to the surface of the salmon. There should also be lots of juice. If you are unsure you may use a fork to check the texture of the salmon. If all else fails, you can always do a taste test. It should be moist yet firm and taste exquisite. If it does, you have been successful.

- Remember, you can always use some spices to help bring out some of the flavour. I usually sprinkle some salt and pepper on the salmon after I make the first turn of the rack. Sometimes I squeeze some lemon juice onto it as well. Remember to keep it simple. If you have a fresh salmon, you shouldn't need to add anything for excellent flavour.

- What kind of salmon? I usually use red spring salmon for best results. It is also a large fish, which ensures you will have enough to feed a good number of people. Another good choice, of course, is sockeye which is one of my favourites.

- Remember that you won't always get it just right. This type of cooking takes practice and you may need time to get a feel for it. It will come to you.

Good luck!
Tyrone Jacobs "Squaw'Le'Kem" Tsawwassen First Nation

Maple Dilled Salmon

Because of my profession, I was once invited to a prison open house. It was during the seventies and I was quite young. My godmother took me, and we didn't bother to check to see if it was maximum, medium or minimum security. I distinctly remember salmon cooking in a pit filled with maple wood. The prisoners were showing us how it was done, and I wish I'd paid more attention. I was too focused on the consumption of the food (a frequent failing) instead of the method of preparation. My brother John assures me that such a pit fire is one of the West Coast's best methods for preparing salmon. I just use the oven.

⅓ cup	butter	75 mL
½ cup	maple syrup	125 mL
1 tsp.	white pepper	5 mL
2	medium onions, sliced	2
6	salmon fillets	6
1 cup	chopped fresh dillweed	250 mL

Melt the butter and add the maple syrup. Mix well. Add pepper and onion slices.

Place salmon fillets in individual sheets of aluminum foil. Pour the maple sauce over the fillets. Sprinkle each fillet with dillweed. Wrap the fillets up tightly and fold to seal so that none of the sauce can escape. Refrigerate for 2 to 3 hours.

Place salmon packets on the barbecue or in a preheated 350°F (180°C) oven. Bake until the salmon is completely done, about 20 minutes per 1" (2.5 cm) of thickness. Serve immediately with Canadian Maple Wild Rice, see page 55.

Serves: 6

John's Maple Salmon Loaf

My brother John is an environmentalist who works to reclaim salmon streams. He and his wildlife biologist friend Matt have successfully returned the salmon to places where they haven't been seen for fifty years. My friend Frank is a vegetarian who can't give up salmon. My son Raymond can eat salmon anywhere, anytime. This recipe was created with all of them in mind.

4 tbsp.	butter OR margarine	60 mL
1	large onion, finely chopped	1
2	celery stalks, finely chopped	2
1	sweet red pepper, finely chopped	1
1 cup	finely chopped mushrooms	250 mL
½ cup	maple syrup	125 mL
2	eggs, beaten	2
2 x 7½ oz.	cans of sockeye salmon, drained	2 x 225 g
1 cup	bread crumbs	250 mL
⅔ cup	skim milk, scalded	150 mL
½ cup	finely chopped dill	125 mL
1 tsp.	pepper	5 mL
½ tsp.	salt	2 mL
4	mushrooms for garnish, sliced	4

Melt the butter in a skillet and sauté the onion, celery, red pepper and mushrooms over medium heat for about 5 to 7 minutes, stirring frequently.

In a large bowl, combine the maple syrup and the eggs with the sautéed vegetables. (Remove the outer skin from the salmon and feed it to your dog, along with the salmon liquid. Our golden retriever, Molly, thinks this is just and equitable.) Add the salmon to the vegetable mixture.

Combine the bread crumbs and the scalded milk. Add to the salmon/vegetable mixture and stir in the dill, pepper and salt.

Place the salmon in a greased 5 x 9" (13 x 23 cm) loaf pan. Garnish with the sliced mushrooms.

Bake, uncovered, at 350°F (180°C) for 1 hour. Let the loaf stand for about 20 minutes before serving.

My son Raymond says this recipe is more "loafy" (read, cuttable) when it sets overnight, refrigerated of course.

Serves: 4 to 6

Maple Ginger Chicken, page 72
Maple Winter Vegetables, page 46

Maple Salmon Mousse

Use only the very best salmon for this. When my oldest son, Matthew, was in kindergarten, we had an "outdoor graduation" reception . . . only in North America. I thought the hostess was a genius because she served this and the kids actually ate it! Use fresh, cooked, red spring salmon, if you can get it.

2 x ¼ oz.	envelopes unflavoured gelatin	2 x 7 g
½ cup	water	125 mL
½ cup	reserved salmon liquid	125 mL
15½ oz.	can sockeye OR red spring salmon, skinned	440 g
½ cup	finely chopped celery	125 mL
½ cup	finely chopped yellow onion	125 mL
¼ cup	finely chopped yellow pepper	60 mL
¼ cup	finely chopped red pepper	60 mL
1 cup	finely chopped fresh cucumber, all seeds removed	250 mL
1 cup	heavy cream	250 mL
½ cup	mayonnaise	125 mL
½ cup	sour cream	125 mL
¼ cup	maple syrup	60 mL
1 tbsp.	chopped fresh dillweed (only feathery parts)	15 mL

Using a small saucepan, sprinkle gelatin over the combined water and salmon liquid. Stir for a minute or so before you turn on the heat to low. Stir constantly, until the gelatin dissolves completely, about 3 minutes.

Place salmon, celery, onion, peppers, cucumber, cream, mayonnaise, sour cream, maple syrup and dillweed in a blender. Process until the mixture is completely smooth, adding the gelatin mixture as you process.

Pour the mixture into a 6-cup (1.5 L) mould, preferably one that looks like a fish. If you have no fish, then place the mousse in a bowl. Chill for about 4 hours. Serve with crackers.

Yield: 6 cups (1.5 L) of lovely Salmon Mousse

Canadian Maple Stew, page 78

Maple Ginger Chicken

This recipe is spectacular for anyone who likes a sweet chicken dish. If you want more sauce, simply double the butter, lemon juice and maple syrup.

¼ cup	vegetable oil	60 mL
4	chicken legs	4
4	chicken thighs	4
4	whole chicken breasts, skinned, boned and halved	4
½ cup	butter	125 mL
⅓ cup	strained lemon juice	75 mL
1 cup	maple syrup	250 mL
¼ cup	chopped crystallized ginger	60 mL
1 tsp.	ground ginger	5 mL
2 tbsp.	cornstarch dissolved in a little water	30 mL
	paprika for garnish	

Heat the oil in a large skillet. Add all of the chicken. I make sure that none of the chicken pieces are too big or too thick. Brown for about 5 minutes over high heat, watching constantly. Transfer drained chicken to another skillet (I use my wok).

Add all of the remaining ingredients, except paprika, to the skillet and bring to a very brief boil. Immediately reduce heat and add the sauce to the chicken. Stir and baste the chicken for a few minutes. Cook, uncovered, for another 30 minutes, until done. Sprinkle with paprika.

Serve with rice or pasta and butternut squash.

Serves: 5

Pictured on page 69.

Maple Sambal Chicken

This dish is a fusion of Indonesian and North American cuisine. It should be served with wild rice, brown rice or short-grained white rice.

2 tbsp.	sambal oelek (crushed chili peppers)	30 mL
⅓ cup	oyster sauce	75 mL
2 tbsp.	sesame seed oil	30 mL
⅓ cup	extra virgin olive oil	75 mL
4	whole chicken breasts, skinned, boned and halved	4
4 tbsp.	butter OR margarine	60 mL
8	fresh OR canned peaches, skinned and sliced	8
½ cup	maple syrup	125 mL
2 cups	whipping cream	500 mL
1 tsp.	turmeric	5 mL
	salt and pepper to taste	
	cooked rice for 6	

Combine sambal oelek, oyster sauce, sesame seed oil and 4 tbsp. (60 mL) of olive oil. Pour this marinade over the chicken and refrigerate for 3 hours.

Remove the chicken from the marinade. Heat the remaining oil and the butter and sauté the chicken for about 2 to 3 minutes on each side. Add the marinade, peaches, maple syrup and cream. Simmer over medium-low heat for about 15 minutes, until the chicken is cooked. Remove the chicken and peaches from the sauce and keep them warm. Stir the turmeric into the cream in the skillet. Return the chicken and peaches to the pan and simmer in the cream sauce for about 3 minutes. Serve over rice.

This dish will be an attractive golden yellow colour. For additional eye appeal and nutritional value, serve this dish with steamed, fresh or frozen green beans or peas.

Serves: 6

Sweet and Sour Maple Chicken

Every recipe with maple syrup in it just tastes better. Try making an entire meal with every dish having maple syrup as one of the ingredients. I guarantee that you will have a happy family and/or happy guests.

4	whole chicken breasts, boned and cubed or slivered	4
¼ cup	vegetable oil	60 mL
3	carrots, sliced	3
1 cup	sliced yellow pepper	250 mL
1 cup	sliced red pepper	250 mL
1 cup	sliced mushrooms (any kind)	250 mL
1	yellow onion, sliced	1
2 cups	chicken broth or bouillon	500 mL
¼ cup	vinegar	60 mL
¼ cup	maple syrup	60 mL
1 tsp.	salt	5 mL
4 tbsp.	cornstarch	60 mL
4 tbsp.	soy sauce	60 mL
½ cup	slivered almonds	125 mL

Heat the oil in a wok or large skillet. Stir in the chicken and stir-fry until it is fully cooked. Set the chicken aside.

Add the carrots, peppers, mushrooms and onion to the skillet. Stir-fry for several minutes. Add chicken broth, vinegar, maple syrup, salt and the cornstarch dissolved in the soy sauce. Add the chicken and cook, covered, for several minutes over medium heat. Check to see if the vegetables are reasonably tender and add the almonds. Serve with brown rice, wild rice or as a filling in crêpes.

Serves: 5 to 6

Sweet and Sour Maple Chicken Wings

These wings don't have a bite but they're loaded with flavour. The sauce, a tart/sweet soy combination, is irresistible.

2 lbs.	chicken wings or drums/drumettes	1 kg
1 cup	flour	250 mL
1 tsp.	salt	5 mL
1 tsp.	pepper	5 mL
2	eggs	2
3 tbsp.	water	45 mL
¼ cup	sunflower oil	60 mL

Maple Sweet and Sour Sauce:

½ cup	vinegar	125 mL
⅔ cup	maple syrup	150 mL
⅓ cup	soy sauce	75 mL
1	onion, finely chopped	1

Separate the chicken wings at the joints. Discard the tips.

Mix the flour, salt and pepper in a bowl. In a separate bowl, mix the eggs and water. Dip the chicken wings into the egg mixture, then into the flour mixture. Heat the oil in a skillet and brown the chicken wings.

Place the wings in a 9 x 13" (23 x 33 cm) baking dish. Combine the vinegar, maple syrup, soy sauce and onion and pour over the chicken wings.

Cover with a lid or aluminum foil.

Temperature: 350°F (180°C)

Baking Time: 1 hour

Serves: 4 (or 1 teenager)

Maple Chicken Parisienne

This is so easy to make and so good – it can be served to company that you really want to impress.

6	skinless chicken breast halves	6
1 tsp.	onion salt	5 mL
1 tbsp.	minced garlic	15 mL
¼ cup	butter	60 mL
1 cup	chopped Portobello mushrooms	250 mL
1	medium-large onion, finely chopped	1
1 cup	sour cream	250 mL
⅔ cup	maple syrup	150 mL
	paprika (optional)	

Place the chicken in a baking pan that will hold it in a single layer. Sprinkle onion salt over the chicken.

In a skillet, heat butter; add mushrooms and onion. Sauté over medium heat for 5 to 7 minutes, until onions are translucent. Spoon the mushroom mixture over the chicken. Combine the sour cream and maple syrup and pour it over the chicken.

Sprinkle with paprika if you so choose.

Temperature: 350°F (180°C)

Baking Time: 1 hour to 1 hour and 15 minutes

Serves: 5

Beef with Portobello Mushrooms
& Maple Whisky Sauce

1½ lbs.	filet of beef, cut into 3 pieces	750 g
6 tbsp.	butter	90 mL
2½ cups	chopped Portobello mushrooms	625 mL

Maple Whisky Sauce:

2 tbsp.	butter	30 mL
4	lean bacon slices, diced	4
5	sprigs fresh parsley	5
1	bay leaf	1
1 tsp.	crushed garlic	5 mL
1	small onion, chopped	1
1 tsp.	fresh thyme	5 mL
¼ cup	butter	60 mL
½ cup	all-purpose flour	125 mL
2 cups	strong beef bouillon	500 mL
1 tsp.	Worcestershire sauce	5 mL
2 tbsp.	butter	30 mL
½ tsp.	freshly ground black pepper	3 mL
1 tsp.	salt	5 mL
¾ cup	maple whisky	175 mL

Sauté beef in 3 tbsp. (45 mL) butter in a large skillet over medium heat, until browned. Allow butter to become quite dark. Set beef aside; add the remaining 3 tbsp. (45 mL) butter and sauté mushrooms for 8 minutes. Keep both warm and do not discard butter or drippings.

To make the sauce, melt butter in a frying pan and add bacon. Add parsley, bay leaf, garlic, onion and thyme. Simmer for about 5 minutes.

In a separate 3-quart (3 L) saucepan, melt ¼ cup (60 mL) butter and stir in flour. Cook the flour until it is dark brown. Add bouillon (if using homemade bouillon, dissolve a beef bouillon cube, such as Knorr or Maggi, into it), a little at a time, stirring constantly. The sauce should be thick at this point. Add the bacon mixture to the sauce and simmer for 30 to 45 minutes. Stir in the Worcestershire sauce, 2 tbsp. (30 mL) butter, pepper, salt and maple whisky.

Serve the sauce hot over the filets. Arrange the mushrooms around the beef and garnish with fresh parsley.

Serves: 6

Canadian Maple Stew

There are few things as comforting on a rainy or snowy evening as walking into a home where a savoury stew is waiting for a hungry family. As Canadians and Americans work harder and harder, trying to hold onto the "American Dream", such evenings are becoming more and more elusive. This stew, made with maple syrup, is relatively low in fat and fantastic when served with fresh, buttered bread and a tossed salad.

3 lbs.	bison OR stewing beef, cubed	1.5 kg
½ cup	all-purpose flour	125 mL
2 cups	chopped butternut OR acorn squash	500 mL
3 cups	diced turnips	750 mL
3	parsnips, peeled and sliced	3
5	carrots, peeled and sliced	5
2	large yellow onions, peeled, cut into quarters	2
2 tbsp.	minced garlic	30 mL
1¼ cups	beef stock	300 mL
1¼ cups	maple syrup*	300 mL
1¼ cups	tomato sauce	300 mL
1 cup	mild tomato OR fruit salsa	250 mL
½ cup	freshly squeezed orange juice	125 mL
1¼ cups	water	300 mL
⅓ cup	chopped fresh dillweed	75 mL
2 tsp.	freshly ground black pepper	10 mL

Dredge the bison or beef cubes with the flour. Place beef and flour in a large roasting pan. Add all remaining ingredients and mix well.

Cover and bake.

Temperature: 325°F (160°C)

Baking Time: 2½ to 3 hours

Serves: 10 adults or 3 teenagers

> * *If you want the stew to be a little less sweet, reduce maple syrup by ½ cup (125 mL) and increase the amount of water by the same amount.*

Pictured on page 70.

aple Chili

This used to be a standard in every diner in North America in the fifties. Then it was called Chili Con Carne but now everyone just seems to call it chili. Aficionados are so crazy about it that there are chili cooking contests across the continent. The distinctive sweetness of maple syrup combines well with the traditional fire of this dish.

3 tbsp.	vegetable oil	45 mL
2 lbs.	extra lean ground beef	1 kg
2 cups	chopped onion	500 mL
2 tbsp.	minced garlic	30 mL
1 cup	sweet green pepper	250 mL
1 cup	sweet red pepper	250 mL
1 cup	sweet yellow pepper	250 mL
1 cup	maple syrup	250 mL
2 cups	sliced or small mushrooms	500 mL
1 cup	tomato sauce	250 mL
1 cup	stewed tomatoes	250 mL
2 x 14 oz.	cans kidney beans	2 x 398 mL
1½ tbsp.	chili powder*	22 mL
	freshly ground black pepper OR white pepper to taste	

Heat the oil in a very large skillet and brown the beef with the onion and garlic until the beef is completely browned and the onions are translucent. Add everything else and simmer, covered, for 1 hour. Uncover and simmer for another 2½ hours.

Serves: 8

* My family does not like "food that hurts", but many people do. If you're a "fire eater", please adjust the amount of chili powder and add hot pepper flakes and/or hot pepper sauce to your taste.

Maple Meatballs in Cream Sauce

This is comfort food, no doubt about it. In the dead of winter, after a long cross-country ski trip, skating party or hard day at work, it's nice not to be exposed to "nouvelle cuisine". Admittedly, the sliver-thin socialites in New York City have been referred to as "social shadows" and this won't make you look like one of them, but you will smile more. Guaranteed.

2 lbs.	extra lean ground beef*	1 kg
2 cups	bread crumbs	500 mL
2 tbsp.	finely chopped fresh parsley	30 mL
2 tbsp.	finely chopped fresh thyme	30 mL
2 tsp.	sea salt	10 mL
⅔ cup	maple syrup	150 mL
2	eggs	2
2 cups	water	500 mL
1½ cups	half and half cream	375 mL
½ cup	all-purpose flour	125 mL
2 cups	beef stock	500 mL
½ cup	vegetable oil	125 mL

Place the beef in a large bowl. Add bread crumbs, parsley, thyme, salt, maple syrup, eggs and ½ cup (125 mL) half and half. Mix everything together with your very clean hands. Roll the meatballs into small, bite-sized portions.

You should end up with about 50 or 60 balls. Dredge meatballs thoroughly with flour. Place oil in a large skillet and cook the meatballs in batches until they are completely done. Each batch should take about 10 minutes on medium heat. They should be nice and brown on the outside and cooked through on the inside. Set cooked meatballs aside.

Add the rest of the flour to the drippings in the skillet, and more oil if you need it. Stir in the water, remaining cream and beef stock. Continue stirring until the sauce boils for a few minutes. Reduce heat to low and add meatballs. Simmer for 15 minutes.

Serve on angel hair spaghetti with freshly steamed garden peas or Blue Lake green beans, if you can get them. Otherwise, just buy a seed packet for next year, haul out your poles and plant the beans next spring.

Serves: 6 to 8

* You may also use ground bison in place of beef.

Marinated Maple Spareribs

You can marinate the spareribs overnight and then cook them in the marinade the next day. These take a long time to prepare because, like the following sparerib recipe, you have to boil the ribs in advance in order to tenderize them. In any event, these are a hit with my boys.

10 lbs.	pork spareribs, cut into single-, 2- or 3-rib portions	4.5 kg

Maple Teriyaki Marinade:

2 cups	teriyaki sauce	500 mL
2 cups	maple syrup	500 mL
1 cup	ketchup	250 mL
½ cup	HP Fruity Sauce	125 mL
1 cup	water	250 mL
1 tbsp.	Worcestershire sauce	15 mL
dash	Tabasco sauce	dash
1 tsp.	garlic powder	5 mL
1	large lemon, juice of	1
1	lemon, thinly sliced	1
⅓ cup	gingered sugar*	75 mL
4 tbsp.	sesame seeds	60 mL
4 tbsp.	cornstarch	60 mL

Trim off all excess fat from the ribs. Boil the ribs in a large pot for 1 hour. You may have to boil them in 2 pots. Discard the water. Place the ribs in a large, deep roasting pan.

Mix all of the marinade ingredients, except the cornstarch, in a large bowl, then pour over the ribs. Marinate, refrigerated, overnight. Cook the next day for the required time. If the sauce is too fluid, add the cornstarch and stir in thoroughly while the ribs are baking.

Serve with rice and Baked Maple Squash, page 47.

Temperature: 350°F (180°C)

Baking Time: 1 hour to 1 hour, 15 minutes

Serves: 8 to 10

> ** Gingered sugar is merely the sugar that falls to the bottom of the bag when you purchase crystallized ginger in the bulk bins. My son Matthew works in a supermarket and he says, "there are always people coming in with cookbooks asking for weird ingredients that we can't find, so make sure you tell your readers what that stuff is because otherwise we'll never find it for them."*

Matthew's Maple Fruit Spareribs

My son Matthew played high school football as a kicker. When the team was losing, he'd comfort himself with the thought that he could dine on these ribs after the game.

7 lbs.	lean pork spare ribs, cut into 2 or 3-rib portions	3 kg

Maple Fruit Barbecue Sauce:

⅓ cup	butter	75 mL
2 tbsp.	minced garlic	30 mL
1 cup	ketchup	250 mL
2 cups	fruit salsa	500 mL
1 cup	pineapple chunks, drained	250 mL
½ cup	chopped candied mango	125 mL
1 cup	maple syrup	250 mL
1 cup	chopped onion	250 mL
2 tbsp.	Worcestershire sauce	30 mL
2 tbsp.	mustard powder	30 mL
2 tsp.	celery seed	10 mL
1 tsp.	salt	5 mL

In a large pot, bring the ribs to a boil. After 15 minutes, reduce heat to medium and boil for another 45 minutes. Remove accumulated scum from time to time and discard. Remove the ribs from the heat. Drain off all water and place the ribs in a large roasting pan.

In a large skillet, melt the butter and add garlic. Sauté for 4 to 5 minutes. Add ketchup, salsa, pineapple, mango, maple syrup, onion, Worcestershire sauce and mustard. Simmer for 10 minutes. Add celery seed and salt.

Pour the sauce over the ribs.

Temperature: 350°F (180°C)

Baking Time: 25 to 30 minutes

Serves: 6 (or 1 football player)

Pictured on page 87.

Maple-Glazed Ham

This recipe is great if you don't want to spend hours in the kitchen on a major holiday. It's also great if you are going to a family potluck, where you have to compete with the other women because you know they'll gossip about you afterwards if you come up with something that, as my children put it, "sucks".

12 lb.	cooked leg of ham	5.5 kg
1¾ cups	orange juice	425 mL
¼ cup	maple whisky	60 mL
1 cup	maple syrup	250 mL
2 tbsp.	Dijon mustard	30 mL
¼ cup	sweet soy sauce	60 mL
	whole cloves for decoration	

Using a very sharp knife, remove the skin from the leg without removing the fat. Cut diamond shapes about 1" (2.5 cm) square on the leg. Do not cut the meat. Place the ham in a large roaster or large shallow baking dish.

In a small saucepan, combine all remaining ingredients, except for the cloves, and heat to melt. Stud the ham with the cloves. Brush the ham with half of the glaze and place in the oven. Baste the ham every 15 minutes during baking with the remaining glaze.

Temperature: 350°F (180°C)

Baking Time: 1½ hours

Serves: 20

Note: If you want to serve fewer people, simply buy a 6 lb. (2.5 kg) ham and keep the glaze recipe the same.

Variation: This ham can also be made with Saskatoon Maple Barbecue Glaze, page 58, Tropical Maple Glaze, page 57 or Maple Whisky Sauce, page 55.

Maple Ham and Pineapple Casserole

The traditional complements of ham and pineapple reach new heights with this zesty vinegar, maple mustard sauce.

3 cups	diced, cooked ham	750 mL
1	large onion, chopped	1
1	large sweet red pepper, chopped	1
1½ cups	fresh or canned pineapple chunks, liquid reserved	375 mL
½ cup	vinegar	125 mL
⅔ cup	maple syrup	150 mL
1 tbsp.	dry mustard	15 mL
3 tbsp.	cornstarch	45 mL
1 tbsp.	teriyaki sauce	15 mL
1 tsp.	Worcestershire sauce	5 mL

Place the ham in the bottom of an ovenproof casserole. Add chopped onions, peppers and pineapple. Place ½ cup (125 mL) of the pineapple juice in a saucepan. Add vinegar and bring to a boil over medium heat. Mix maple syrup, mustard and cornstarch in a bowl. Stir into the pineapple juice. Cook over medium heat until thick. Remove from heat and add teriyaki sauce and Worcestershire sauce. Pour the maple/pineapple sauce over the ham mixture and bake.

Serve with rice.

Temperature: 350°F (180°C)

Baking Time: 45 minutes

Serves: 4

Maple
&
Fruit

 Maple Syrup

Sweetener with a conscience – A little history, a little politics.

The entire European consumption of sugar for the year 1600 could easily have been contained in one bulk carrier. Before that, when the glories of the European Renaissance were being created, the average sugar consumption was roughly one teaspoon (five millilitres) per head per year. Today, tens of millions of people eat four to five pounds (two kilograms) of sugar per week.

Europe's voracious appetite for sugar created a huge demand for labour. Caribbean and American plantation owners, anxious to meet the growing demand, placed larger and larger tracts of land under cultivation for sugar cane. The harvest of this important commodity exacted an awful toll on the black workers who were forcibly removed from Africa and brought to the West Indies, and then America, and commanded to cut the cane. Yellow fever, malaria, snake bites, heat prostration, this was their awful fate.

In *Seeds of Change, Five Seeds That Transformed Mankind*, author Henry Hobhouse discusses how the slave trade to America had been kick-started by colonialists centuries before. In 1514, explorer Bartolome Las Casas was granted a block of land in the Spanish colony of Cuba. The block of land came with roughly one hundred Amerindian Caribs attached to it. The concept of slaves or "chattels" made it possible for landowners to leave the brutally hard work to the slaves. Las Casas was no different. He tried, with no luck, to get the gentle Arawaks, another Caribbean tribe, to do the work. The Caribs were even more reluctant. They were aggressive meat eaters and, in the 1520s, they had demonstrated their reluctance to be enslaved by sticking two Spanish landowners in the pot and eating them. Both the Arawaks and the Caribs simply resisted enslavement by pining away and dying.

Continued on page 89.

Matthew's Maple Fruit Spareribs, page 82

Oven-Roasted Maple Onion Potatoes, page 50

Maple Carrots, Leek & Cauliflower, page 46

 Maple Syrup
(continued)

Las Casas suggested the African Negro would be a suitable alternative for the slavery that was required for the sugar harvest. They were known to be exceptionally strong and hard workers. His suggestion effectively sealed the fate of millions of blacks. Las Casas died regretting his choice. In an attempt to rescue his soul, he became a priest and championed the rights of Indians and blacks. But it was too late. The trans-Atlantic slave trade had begun and the international appetite for sugar had become insatiable.

In the nineteenth century, every teaspoon of sugar represented six days of the life of a black slave. Of course, abolitionists began to speak up and maple sugar and syrup made their politically correct debut. In 1824, William Drown, an American, stated in his *Compendium of Agriculture* that:

> *The cane sugar is the result of the forced labour of the most wretched slaves, toiling under the cruel lash of a cutting whip. While the maple sugar is made by those who are happy and free.*

In England, a china warehouse's advertisement for sugar containers reflected the wave of abolitionist thought. A message on each container proclaimed that the sugar it contained was not made by slaves. The firm's advertisement indicated how many black lives would be saved by not using cane sugar from the West Indies (now the Caribbean). It added that eight families using maple sugar for a period of twenty years could save the lives of one hundred blacks.

The Northern United States was heavily involved in the "underground railway", the name used for the conduit of people and places that helped slaves escape from the Southern plantations. Maine and Vermont, as northern states, were large growers of maple trees and, hence, as producers of maple syrup they became known as prime producers of this "sweetener with a conscience".

So it was that the maple tree became a symbol of the moral higher ground. Today, maple syrup is considered a luxury and is sold in airports, cruise ships, gift stores and supermarkets all over North America. In Europe and Asia, for those lucky enough to get it, it is a gourmet treat. The association with the moral high ground has faded into history.

Peter Stuyvesant Maple Fruit Salad, page 91

Larissa's Maple Tropical Salad

My daughter, Larissa, is always fighting her weight. She eats in moderation and exercises in order to stay in shape. You can always convince her to eat fruit and, because she loves Mexico and anything tropical, this salad is for her.

1 cup	lychee fruit*	250 mL
1 cup	sliced bananas	250 mL
2 cups	sliced mangoes	500 mL
2 cups	fresh blueberries	500 mL
1½ cups	pineapple chunks	375 mL
1 cup	sliced ripe papaya	250 mL
1 cup	slivered almonds	250 mL
⅔ cup	maple syrup	150 mL

Prepare the fruit and combine with almonds and syrup. Mix well and serve. This salad looks beautiful in a clear glass bowl.

Serves: 6 to 8

* *Also spelled litchi or lichee, this fruit has been popular in southeast Asia, especially in China, for over 2,000 years. Available, fresh, canned or dried, the fresh fruit is usually in season in June and July. The dried fruits are often called lychee nuts because they look like nuts, with brownish shells and flesh.*

Peter Stuyvesant Maple Fruit Salad

My papa was a historian so at our dinner table it was a normal thing to discuss stuff like the exact date that Jacques Cartier first sailed into the St. Lawrence, where Samuel de Champlain wintered and why Peter Stuyvesant lost New York, as well as his leg, to the English. Other kids thought I was crazy for caring about such things.

2	bananas, peeled and thickly sliced	2
2	peaches, peeled and sliced	2
	lemon juice	
2 cups	hulled, sliced strawberries	500 mL
2 cups	sliced mango	500 mL
2	kiwifruit, peeled and sliced	2
1 cup	fresh raspberries	250 mL
2 cups	blueberries	500 mL
1 cup	maple syrup	250 mL
½ cup	maple whisky	125 mL
½ cup	maple cream liqueur	125 mL
2 cups	whipping cream (optional)	500 mL
6 tbsp.	icing sugar OR maple syrup	75 mL
1 pkg.	Dr. Oetker's Whipit (optional)	1 pkg.

Sprinkle the banana and peach slices with lemon juice to preserve colour. Add all remaining fruit and combine in a large attractive salad bowl. (Crystal shows off the fruit to great advantage.) Mix the maple syrup with the maple whisky and maple cream liqueur and pour over the fruit. Chill until serving time. Make this salad on the day you want to serve it because the softer berries "don't travel well".

If you choose, whip the cream and sweeten with either maple syrup or icing sugar. If not serving immediately, you may want to add the Whipit stabilizer. Serve the whipped cream in a separate crystal bowl.

This is a beautifully simple, yet elegant dessert. This fruit salad is also lovely for a fashionable brunch.

Serves: 10 to 12

Pictured on page 88.

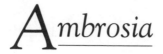Ambrosia

My mama makes this all the time, except she calls it Five-Cup Salad. She imported this recipe from American friends during the fifties. It's the kind of recipe that women have been making for years when they need something for a dessert and they have only ten minutes in which to make it. It seems to work because, when she makes it, there's never any left and everyone's always looking for more.

1 cup	mandarin orange segments, drained	250 mL
1 cup	pineapple bits or chunks, drained	250 mL
1 cup	shredded, sweetened coconut	250 mL
1 cup	whipping cream (not whipped)	250 mL
1 cup	mini marshmallows	250 mL
¼ cup	maple syrup	60 mL

Prepare the fruit and combine all of the ingredients in a crystal bowl. Refrigerate for about 2 to 3 hours before serving.

Serves: 4 to 6

Note: You can also make this the night before, but cover it with plastic wrap so no odours migrate to the cream.

Blueberry Maple Ice Cream

Fresh blueberries and maple syrup, this is so good and so easy.

2	eggs	2
⅔ cup	maple sugar	150 mL
1 cup	whole milk	250 mL
1 tbsp.	maple syrup liqueur	15 mL
2 tbsp.	maple syrup	30 mL
1½ cups	whipping cream, chilled	375 mL
4 cups	puréed fresh blueberries	1 L

Beat eggs lightly. Add sugar slowly and beat for 1 to 2 minutes. In a saucepan, heat milk until it is almost boiling. Add the milk to the egg mixture and mix well. Cool and then add maple liqueur, maple syrup, whipping cream and blueberries. Pour the maple cream mixture into an ice cream maker and follow directions.

Serves: 6 to 8

Maple Macadamia Ice Cream

This combination of macadamia and maple syrup is rich, creamy and oh, so satisfying.

2 cups	whipping cream, chilled	500 mL
1 cup	whole milk	250 mL
1⅓ cups	maple syrup	325 mL
5	egg yolks, beaten	5
1 tbsp.	maple syrup liqueur	15 mL
1 cup	chopped macadamia nuts	250 mL

Place whipping cream, milk and maple syrup in a saucepan and warm over low heat until it is hot. DO NOT BOIL. Stir in beaten egg yolks and then add maple liqueur. Pour the maple cream mixture into an ice cream maker and process. When the ice cream is done, stir in the macadamia nuts and freeze.

Serves: 6

Variation: For **Maple Pecan Ice Cream**, substitute pecans for macadamia nuts.

Strawberry Maple Cream

It's difficult to resist a dish like this so just content yourself with the fact that the strawberries have a lot of Vitamin C and get on with it. This is especially nice if you have lovely small strawberries in your garden. The really big ones that you purchase in the supermarket often seem to be distinctly lacking in flavour. You have to do too much to them to make them taste like strawberries.

2 cups	small strawberries	500 mL
⅓ cup	maple sugar OR maple syrup	75 mL
¼ cup	maple cream liqueur	60 mL
1¼ cups	whipping cream	300 mL
3 tbsp.	maple sugar	45 mL

Reserve about 10 strawberries for decoration. Place the remaining strawberries in a medium-sized bowl and crush with a potato masher or with a large fork or blend in a blender. Add maple syrup and mix well.

Whip maple cream liqueur, whipping cream and maple sugar until the cream holds stiff peaks. Fold in mashed strawberries. Spoon Strawberry Cream into individual dessert dishes or parfait glasses. Garnish with fresh, whole berries with hull attached.

Serves: 4 to 6

Pictured on page 106.

Mango Maple Meringues

These are spectacular and very versatile. Make individual meringues or, if you really want to impress your guests, one large meringue.

8	egg whites	8
½ tsp.	cream of tartar	2 mL
2 cups	berry/superfine sugar (finely granulated sugar)	500 mL
1 tbsp.	maple cream liqueur	15 mL

Preheat oven to 250°F (120°C). Cover 1 or 2 large cookie sheets with baking parchment.

Beat the egg whites with an electric mixer on low until frothy. Add the cream of tartar and continue beating until the egg whites form soft peaks. Add the sugar very, very slowly so that it is totally incorporated into the egg whites. Continue beating until the sugar is dissolved and white, shiny peaks form. Beat the maple cream liqueur in last, also adding it very slowly.

Make individual meringues by spooning the paste onto the cookie sheet(s) to make 20 nests. Use 2 spoons to shape the nests. OR, place the meringue paste into a pastry bag and, using a star tip and a circular motion, make a circular base with a 10" (25 cm) circumference. To make a circle, trace the outer edge of a pie plate, face down. You can create a circular nest or you can create an edge on the meringue by squeezing little rosettes all around the circumference of the meringue. Dry the meringue in the preheated oven.

Baking Time: 1 hour. Leave the meringue in the oven for an additional hour after the heat has been turned off (with the oven door closed).

Fill the meringues with the Mango Maple Filling, page 95.

Yield: approximately 20 small nests or 1 large meringue

Note: I like meringues best if they are served the next day but you can store them for longer if you like. Some people buy meringues, but I find the ones you make yourself are better. The above meringue recipe can also serve for a Pavlova if you make 1 large meringue.

Mango Maple Meringues
(continued)

Mango Maple Filling:

8 cups	sliced mango	2 L
2 cups	fresh blueberries (optional)	500 mL
½ cup	maple syrup	125 mL
1 qt.	Maple Macadamia ice cream, frozen very hard (see page 93)	1 L

Combine the fruit and maple syrup. Place small meringues on individual plates or the large meringue on a serving platter. With a melon scoop or ice-cream scoop, scoop ice cream into the meringue nest(s). Spoon the Mango Filling decoratively over the ice cream.

Serves: 10 to 12

Variation: Fruit sorbets or sherbets make beautiful and delicious substitutions for the ice cream.

Pictured on page 105.

Maple Mudslide

During the sixties there was a little place called The Fourth Dimension, a coffee house in Winnipeg, Manitoba. A lot of rock bands had their start there but, of course, what I remember was the food. They used to serve concoctions similar to Maple Mudslide. This is in memory of some of their spectacular creations.

8 scoops	Maple Pecan Ice Cream (see page 93)	8 scoops
2 cups	tempered dark Dutch chocolate (see tempering instructions on page 148)	500 mL
3 tbsp.	butter	45 mL
5 ripe	mangoes, peeled and sliced	5
3 cups	fresh blueberries	750 mL
1⅓ cups	chopped macadamia nuts	325 mL

Place individual servings of the maple pecan ice cream in serving dishes.

Temper chocolate in the top part of a double boiler. Add butter, melt and mix well. Pour or spoon the chocolate over the ice cream. Add mango slices, blueberries and sprinkle with macadamia nuts.

Serves: 8

Strawberry Maple Syrup Parfait

Turkey Hill Sugarbush Ltd. is a company in Waterloo, Québec, Canada that ships maple syrup products all over the world. Their excellent products can be found in airports, gift stores and many other venues where really "good stuff" is sold. President Brian Herman tells me that demand is increasing as the world discovers this exquisite delicacy, and also discovers that it is accessible. This recipe is courtesy of Mr. Herman's company.

1 cup	pure maple syrup	250 mL
3	egg yolks	3
2 cups	whipping cream, whipped	500 mL
3	egg whites, stiffly beaten	3
	sliced strawberries	
	white rum (optional)	

Heat the maple syrup in a double boiler. Beat the egg yolks well and add slowly to the syrup, stirring constantly. When the mixture thickens, allow it to cool. Add whipped cream and stiffly beaten egg whites.

Turn into a soufflé dish and refrigerate for several hours. Garnish with sliced strawberries and sprinkle generously with rum.

Serves: 4 to 6 happy guests

Papa's Maple Apples

When I was little, my mama made dessert every night of the week, 365 days per year. My papa and I NEVER turned down any dessert. My papa always appreciated Mama's cooking, and they were married for 60 years. When Alzheimer's claimed my papa's brilliance, he'd still go for the sweets like an eagle for its prey. When he died, my brother John and I were comforted by the fact that Papa had waited until after breakfast to die.

6	Granny Smith apples, cored	6
1 cup	raisins	250 mL
1 cup	slivered almonds	250 mL
2 tsp.	cinnamon	10 mL
1 cup	maple syrup	250 mL
	butter	

Core the apples in such a way that there is a "floor" to the apple. In other words, don't hollow it out all the way to the bottom but do remove the seeds and core.

Place the apples in a baking pan and stuff each apple with raisins and almonds. Sprinkle the filling in each apple with some cinnamon and pour maple syrup into each hole. Pat a dab of butter over the fillings. Baste apples once or twice while they are baking.

Temperature: 350°F (180°C)

Baking Time: 40 to 60 minutes, depending on the apple size. When baked they should still be slightly firm.

Serves: 6

Chocolate Maple Pears

Pears and chocolate are already a heavenly combination, and the maple cream liqueur only makes it better.

| 2 cups | water | 500 mL |
| 6 | Anjou pears, peeled and cored | 6 |

Chocolate Maple Sauce:

¼ cup	butter	60 mL
¼ cup	maple syrup	60 mL
¼ cup	Dutch cocoa	60 mL
1 tbsp.	maple cream liqueur	15 mL

Place the water in a pot with a steaming basket. Bring to a boil. Peel and core pears. Cut pears in half and steam for 5 to 8 minutes, until tender.

To make the sauce, melt butter in a skillet. Add maple syrup and sprinkle in cocoa. Incorporate completely. Add liqueur and simmer for a minute.

Place the pears on attractive serving dishes and pour Chocolate Maple Sauce over each serving. Serve immediately.

Serves: 6 (in a normal household – 3 at ours)

Maple Whisky Peaches

Brandied Peaches are a traditional treat, but peaches macerated in maple whisky are truly succulent.

	water	
6	ripe peaches	6
	lemon juice, strained	
⅓ cup	maple sugar	75 mL
⅓ cup	maple whisky OR maple cream liqueur	75 mL

Maple Whisky Peaches
(continued)

Pour water into a medium saucepan and allow to come to a boil. Place the peaches into the boiling water for about 30 to 40 seconds and remove. Transfer the hot peaches to cold water and remove the skins. Place the peaches in a serving bowl and sprinkle with lemon juice to prevent discolouration. Prick peaches with a fork.

In a small saucepan, mix the maple sugar and maple whisky. Heat, stirring constantly, until the sugar dissolves. Do not allow it to come to a boil. Pour the whisky sauce over the peaches.

Cover the serving bowl with plastic wrap and refrigerate the peaches for about 4 hours prior to serving, to allow flavours to blend.

Serve individual peaches in attractive serving dishes. Serve with a rich vanilla ice cream or custard, if you wish.

Serves: 6

Bananas Flambé

This is the kind of recipe that you can prepare in front of your guests in a chafing dish – only if you are a flamboyant cook and a risk taker. I wouldn't do it because I don't have that kind of lifestyle and I'd probably set the house on fire.

¼ cup	butter	60 mL
6	medium, ripe bananas, peeled and cut in half lengthwise	6
½ cup	packed maple sugar	125 mL
⅓ cup	maple whisky OR maple cream liqueur	75 mL
½ cup	toasted slivered almonds	125 mL

Melt butter in a medium-sized skillet. Add bananas and sauté until they are golden. Sprinkle the maple sugar over the bananas and add the maple whisky or liqueur.

Bring the whisky mixture to a boil and ignite. Shake the skillet over the heat until the flames die.

Place 2 banana halves in each of 6 serving dishes and garnish with toasted almonds.

Serves: 6

Crêpes Maple Melba

Be adventurous. Escoffier created Melba Sauce, for the famous Australian opera diva Dame Nellie Melba, using raspberries. For this Northern Hemisphere version I use strawberries and maple sugar with the traditional peaches and ice cream and wrap them all in a warm crêpe.

10 oz.	pkg. frozen, sweetened strawberries	284 g
1 tbsp.	cornstarch	15 mL
2 tbsp.	water	30 mL
¼ cup	maple sugar OR maple syrup	60 mL
4	fresh peaches, peeled and sliced	4
	vanilla ice cream	
6-8	crêpes (see recipe for Johnny's Skinny Pancakes on page 15)	6-8

Defrost strawberries and place them in a medium saucepan. Bring to a boil, stirring continuously. Mash the berries with a fork as you stir. Dissolve cornstarch in water and add to the strawberries. Stir in maple sugar or maple syrup and dissolve. Add peaches and mix thoroughly

Meanwhile, place warm crêpes on attractive serving plates and spoon the strawberry-peach mixture onto the crêpes. Roll up the crêpes and spoon vanilla ice cream over them. Serve immediately.

Serves: 4

Maple Macadamia Granny Crunch

If you think about how well trees serve us on this planet, it's hard not to have an immense gratitude. This is especially true for those of us who like to eat. When you think "maple tree" and "apple tree" and then "macadamia tree", it's enough to give a poet material for ten years. Enough said. Here's what happens when the Granny Smith apple tree, the maple tree and the macadamia tree team up.

6 cups	peeled, sliced Granny Smith apples	1.5 L
⅓ cup	all-purpose flour	75 mL
1 cup	brown sugar	250 mL
⅔ cup	maple syrup	150 mL
1 tsp.	maple syrup liqueur	5 mL
2 tsp.	cinnamon	10 mL

Oatmeal Maple Macadamia Topping:

2¼ cups	rolled oats	550 mL
1¼ cups	all-purpose flour	300 mL
⅔ cup	maple syrup	150 mL
¾ cup	butter, melted	175 mL
1½ tsp.	baking powder	7 mL
1½ tsp.	baking soda	7 mL
1 cup	chopped macadamia nuts	250 mL

In a large bowl, combine the apples, flour, sugar, maple syrup, maple liqueur and cinnamon. Pour into a 9 x 12" (23 x 30 cm) baking pan.

Combine all of the topping ingredients and spread gently over the apple mixture.

Temperature: 350°F (180°C)

Baking Time: 35 minutes

Serves: 8 to 10

Blueberry Maple Crunch

In the shadows of Vancouver's business towers, the verdant Fraser Valley fights a valiant battle against rapid urbanization. In Pitt Meadows, British Columbia, Patrick and Joanne Freeman's beautiful blueberry farm yields tons of lovely blueberries that never see a supermarket. They're all sold within hours of picking. Those blueberries are loaded with "good stuff" and Patrick will tell anyone who wants to hear.

Oatmeal Cinnamon Crust:

3 cups	rolled oats	750 mL
1 cup	cake/pastry flour	250 mL
½ cup	unsalted butter, melted	125 mL
2 tsp.	cinnamon	10 mL

Blueberry Maple Filling:

1	egg	1
1 cup	sour cream	250 mL
¾ cup	maple syrup	175 mL
3 tbsp.	cornstarch	45 mL
1 tsp.	cinnamon	5 mL
1 tbsp.	maple cream liqueur	15 mL
3 cups	fresh or frozen blueberries	750 mL

To make the crust, combine oatmeal, cake flour, melted butter and cinnamon. Grease a 9" (23 cm) square pan and press half of the crust mixture over the bottom of the pan.

To make the filling, beat the egg with the sour cream. In a separate bowl, mix the maple syrup gradually with the cornstarch. Stir in the cinnamon and liqueur. Stir in the sour cream mixture and the blueberries. Place the blueberry mixture on top of the crumb crust and sprinkle with the remaining crumbs.

Temperature: 325°F (165°C)

Baking Time: 1 hour

Serves: 8

To serve, top with Blueberry Maple Ice Cream, page 92.

Note: If you like sweet crusts, simply add ½ cup (125 mL) maple sugar to the oatmeal crust.

Maple Cream Blueberry Trifle

You can tell a host or hostess who has skimped on trifle ingredients from the very first bite. I have walked away from more trifles because the ingredients were sub-standard and not worth the considerable calories. If you are going to indulge, you might as well do it on first-class calories.

1	pound cake* (purchased or baked according to recipe on page 138)	1
½ cup	maple cream liqueur	125 mL
1 cup	blueberry OR saskatoon jam	250 mL
2 cups	vanilla custard**	500 mL
2 cups	fresh blueberries OR saskatoons	500 mL
2 cups	sliced fresh strawberries	500 mL
2 cups	whipping cream	500 mL
2 tbsp.	maple sugar OR maple syrup	30 mL
1 tbsp.	maple whisky	15 mL
½ cup	slivered almonds, toasted	125 mL
½ cup	fresh blueberries	125 mL
½ cup	sliced fresh strawberries	125 mL

Line the bottom and sides of a 3-quart (3 L) glass trifle dish with about half of the sponge cake. Create a tight fit and paint all sponge cake surfaces with half of the maple cream liqueur. Spread blueberry or saskatoon jam over the cake. Use about three-quarters of the jam.

Layer half of the vanilla custard over the jam-covered cake and sprinkle with half of the blueberries and strawberries. Place the rest of the cake on top of the berries. Paint the remaining cake with the remaining maple liqueur and spread with the remaining jam. Sprinkle the rest of the blueberries and strawberries over the cake. Top with the remaining custard and cover with plastic wrap to prevent the custard from developing a "skin".

You can let the trifle set for 3 to 4 days but I prefer to serve it within 12 to 15 hours. Before serving, whip the whipping cream with the maple sugar or maple syrup until it forms peaks. Cover the trifle completely with the whipped cream and garnish with the toasted almonds, blueberries and strawberries.

Serves: 10 to 12

* *You can use frozen Sara Lee Pound Cake for this recipe. It works well.*

** *See Maple Custard, page 118, or you can use cooked vanilla pudding for this recipe, but be sure to use homogenized milk. NEVER use instant pudding.*

Maple Mango Cheesecake

I really like the concept of the gifts from the trees of the Northern Hemisphere blended with the gifts from the trees of the Southern Hemisphere.

Ginger Crumb Crust:

1¼ cups	gingersnaps	300 mL
¼ cup	sugar	60 mL
¼ cup	unsalted butter	60 mL

Maple Mango Filling:

3 x 8 oz.	packages cream cheese, softened	3 x 250 g
14 oz.	can sweetened condensed milk	396 g
2 cups	mashed, ripe mango	500 mL
3	large eggs	3
¼ cup	maple syrup	60 mL

Maple Almond Glaze:

¾ cup	maple syrup	175 mL
1 cup	whipping cream	250 mL
½ cup	slivered almonds, toasted	125 mL

Mix gingersnaps, sugar and unsalted butter in a medium-sized bowl. Mix well and press into the bottom of a 9" (23 cm) springform pan.

Beat the cream cheese at medium speed with an electric mixer until the cream cheese is fluffy. Add the sweetened condensed milk. Beat until smooth. Add the mango, eggs and maple syrup. Blend completely and pour the filling over the crust.

Temperature: 300°F (150°C)

Baking Time: 1 hour to 1 hour and 15 minutes, or until completely set

The cheesecake should generally "rest" overnight prior to serving.

To make the glaze, bring syrup and whipping cream to a boil in a medium-sized saucepan. Boil, stirring occasionally, for about 10 minutes, until thickened. Stir in the almonds and pour over the cheesecake. Serve immediately.

Serves: 10 to 12

Mango Maple Meringues, page 94

Maple
Candies
&
Puddings

Strawberry Maple Cream, page 93

107

The Maple Tree: Yesterday and Today

The maple tree wasn't always considered the source of gourmet treats as it is today. The indigenous people of what was then Upper Canada, Lower Canada and the New England states used maple syrup and maple sugar almost exclusively as an enhancer and as a staple. They did not like salt. They would add large quantities of maple syrup to meat and corn, their staple diets. Sometimes they would eat nothing but maple sugar for weeks at a time. They loved the brownish maple sugar and grew fat on it. When they first saw the refined white sugar that the French brought from their homeland, they thought it odd and referred to it as "French snow". The French settlers quickly adopted native ways of harvesting this important commodity. In 1751, Pehr Kalm wrote:

> The common people in the northernmost English colonies, as well as the French in Canada, supply themselves with a large quantity of this sugar each year. Many farmers have whole barrels full for their own use. Practically every soldier in the French forts manufactures a year's supply of this necessity for himself in the spring. If you visit the French, you will see no other sugar used. When milk is served, it is heavily flavoured with maple sugar, and the sugar bowl is placed on the table so everyone can sweeten his food according to his taste.

The maple tree is a hardwood that is slow in its growth. There are many, many kinds of maple trees that grow across the North American continent. Sap can be harvested from almost all of them, but the primary sources of maple syrup and sugar are the rock or sugar maple and the black maple.

The maple tree is an inspiration for all who let it touch their souls. "Leaf peepers" from all over the world phone New England's "leaf hotlines" to find out when the majestic maple foliage will be at its most brilliant. Tourists book months in advance, filling hotels in the New England states, Québec and Ontario to capacity. The maple leaf is such a powerful symbol that it graces the flag of Canada, the national news desks and constitutes the logo of countless corporations, including a national hockey team. Any Canadian who is in a foreign airport, and sees the giant maple leaf on a black background proudly etched on the tail of an Air Canada jet, immediately yearns for home and all that implies. Around the world, young Canadians wear the maple leaf on backpacks and clothes to announce their country of origin.

This book is a tribute to the maple tree, a tree that can produce a quarter of a million or more glorious leaves, can provide shade in the summer, beautiful wood for hardwood floors and furniture that will last for centuries, inspiration for poets, writers, corporations, nations, and, lastly, it provides us with the "Season of the Maple Moon" during which we can all celebrate the flow of this nectar of the gods.

Manitoba Maple Creams

When I was a little girl, we moved from the Netherlands to Manitoba, Canada. We had Manitoba maple trees and, in the spring, the sap would run. I was one of those kids who would get her tongue stuck to frozen bridges and railway tracks so it's not surprising that I licked the trunks of those trees. I can still remember the surprise I felt when I discovered the sweetness of that sap. Today, small cottage operations harvest the sap from those Manitoba maples and produce excellent results.

2 cups	maple syrup*	500 mL
3 tbsp.	corn syrup	45 mL
2 cups	cream	500 mL
2 cups	dark brown sugar	500 mL
3 tbsp.	unsalted butter	45 mL
1 tbsp.	maple cream whisky	15 mL

Butter the sides of a large saucepan. Add the maple syrup, corn syrup, cream, sugar and butter and bring to a gentle boil. Stir until the syrup begins to boil, then cover for about 3 minutes. Bring to the soft ball stage, 234°F (112°C).

Stir in the maple cream whisky.

Remove the maple cream from the heat and beat until thick and creamy. Pour into individual candy moulds or a greased 8 x 8" (20 x 20 cm) pan.

Yield: 24 pieces of fudge

* In testing this recipe, I must confess I used Québec maple syrup.

Maple Nut Brittle

This brittle was developed by Jeremy Stevens of the Great Canadian Fudge Company in Maple Ridge, British Columbia, Canada. Maple Ridge is located in the beautiful Fraser Valley where Jeremy and his wife, Donna, develop the recipes for their fudge. As wholesale manufacturers, they supply duty-free shops, ice cream and gift stores as well as candy stores from Victoria, British Columbia on the West Coast, to Baddeck, Nova Scotia on the East Coast.

⅓ cup	plus 2 tbsp. (30 mL) water	100 mL
1⅓ cups	corn syrup OR glucose	325 mL
3⅔ cups	sugar	900 mL
4 tbsp.	of butter	60 mL
5 cups	chopped nuts (use pecans, cashews OR almonds)	1.25 L
1 tbsp.	baking soda	15 mL
2 tbsp.	maple syrup	30 mL

In a large, stainless steel saucepan over medium heat, combine water, corn syrup and sugar. Turn up the heat and stir.

Dissolve sugar and then add butter. Stir constantly. When the temperature reaches 260°F (120°F) on a candy thermometer, add the nuts.

Keep the temperature on high and don't stop stirring. Take the mixture up to 290 to 295°F (145°C) and then remove from the heat. Add baking soda and syrup and stir in quickly. Be careful as it will bubble up. Allow the mixture to rise until it is 2" (5 cm) from the top of the pot and then stir it back down.

Line 2 large cookie sheets with parchment paper. Pour the nut brittle mixture onto the paper. Spread as thinly as possible. Cool. When it is okay to touch, start breaking up the brittle. It MUST be totally cooled before storing. Store in an airtight container.

Yield: about 2 lbs. (1 kg) of brittle

Crunchy Maple Jungle Bark

This is another great candy to make all year round. It's really hard to resist.

¼ cup	chopped cashews	60 mL
¼ cup	chopped macadamia nuts	60 mL
½ cup	sweetened coconut	125 mL
10 oz.	semisweet Dutch OR Belgian chocolate	285 g
¼ cup	chopped dried papaya	60 mL
¼ cup	chopped dried mango	60 mL
3 tbsp.	maple syrup	45 mL
1 tbsp.	maple cream liqueur	15 mL
½ cup	crushed banana chips	125 mL

Place the cashews, macadamia nuts and coconut on a baking sheet sprayed lightly with non-stick spray. Bake on the lowest rack in a 200°F (93°C) oven for about 3 to 5 minutes. DON'T leave it – keep your eye on the nut mixture and when it turns golden, remove it immediately.

Melt the chocolate in a double boiler. When the chocolate is completely liquefied, remove from heat and add nuts and coconut. Stir in all of the remaining ingredients until completely mixed.

Place parchment paper on a baking sheet and spread the chocolate/fruit mixture over the parchment paper. Once the bark has cooled, break it into chunks. Alternatively, you can drop spoonfuls of the chocolate/fruit mixture onto the parchment paper, like drop cookies. Store cooled bark in an airtight container.

Yield: 1 pound (250 g) of candy

Maple Turtles

This is a great treat to make as a Christmas gift for your friends.

1 lb.	Belgian OR Dutch milk chocolate, tempered (see tempering instructions on page 148)	500 g
1½ cups	whipping cream	375 mL
¼ cup	white sugar	60 mL
¼ cup	maple syrup	60 mL
½ cup	brown sugar	125 mL
¾ cup	corn syrup	175 mL
½ tsp.	salt	2 mL
1 tbsp.	maple whisky	15 mL
4 tbsp.	unsalted butter	60 mL
3 cups	pecans	750 mL

Melt the chocolate in a double boiler and temper it according to the instructions on page 148.

Combine half of the cream and all of the white sugar, maple syrup, brown sugar, corn syrup and salt in a large saucepan. Stir the sugar mixture frequently and bring it to 234°F (115°C). Add the remaining cream slowly and then allow the temperature to rise to 244°F (120°C). Remove the sugar mixture from the heat and immediately stir in the maple whisky and unsalted butter.

Place baking parchment on 4 cookie sheets and place 4 or 5 pecans in clusters on the cookie sheets at intervals. Pour some of the caramel mixture over each pecan cluster and allow them to cool. Then pour the chocolate over the caramel clusters and cool again.

Yield: 40 to 50 maple turtles

Maple Macadamia Chocolate Fudge

When you are trying to observe Lent and abstain from sweets, don't make this fudge. This recipe has successfully tempted many.

½ cup	brown sugar	125 mL
1½ cups	maple syrup	375 mL
¾ cup	semisweet, dark Dutch OR Belgian chocolate	175 mL
¾ cup	evaporated milk	175 mL
½ tsp.	salt	2 mL
3 tbsp.	unsalted butter	45 mL
1 tbsp.	maple cream liqueur	15 mL
1 cup	halved macadamia nuts	250 mL

Combine the brown sugar and maple syrup in a heavy, buttered saucepan. Cook slowly over low to medium heat. Be careful to avoid scorching.

Melt the chocolate separately, in a double boiler, and add to the syrup mixture. Add milk and salt. Bring to the softball stage, between 234°F and 240°F (112 to 115°C) on a candy thermometer.

Remove the fudge from the heat and immediately add the butter and maple cream liqueur. Continue stirring and add the macadamia nuts. Spread in a greased, 8" (20 cm) pan.

Cut the cooled fudge, after it sets, with a sharp knife dipped in hot water.

Yield: about 24 pieces of fudge

Maple Chocolate Crisps

Raisins and mango are an irresistible combination, especially when teamed up with chocolate and maple.

1 cup	dark raisins	250 mL
4 tbsp.	maple cream liqueur OR maple syrup liqueur	60 mL
14 oz.	semisweet Dutch chocolate	400 g
1 cup	slivered almonds	250 mL
¼ cup	finely chopped candied mango	60 mL

Place the raisins in a small mixing bowl and toss with the maple cream liqueur. Cover and allow to steep overnight.

Line a baking sheet with parchment paper. Temper the chocolate according to the instructions on page 148. Cool slightly and then add to the raisin and maple cream liqueur mixture. Add almonds and candied mango.

Use a large spoon and place mounds of the candy mixture onto the parchment paper. Place in the refrigerator and allow the candy to cool.

Store the cooled crisps in an airtight container.

Yield: 2 dozen candies

Variation: Substitute chopped dried apricots for the mango if you prefer.

Maple Popcorn

With the price of popcorn at theatres today, it's a better idea to rent a movie, prepare this treat and stay home. This popcorn tastes even better on very cold winter nights.

12 cups	popped corn	3 L
⅓ cup	maple syrup	75 mL
½ cup	butter	125 mL
½ cup	dark brown sugar	125 mL
½ cup	light brown sugar	125 mL
¼ tsp.	baking soda	1 mL
1 tsp.	maple whisky	5 mL
¼ cup	chopped pecans	60 mL
¼ cup	chopped almonds	60 mL

Spray a large roasting pan with non-stick spray. Place the popcorn in the roasting pan and set it aside.

Place maple syrup, butter and sugars in a saucepan and bring to a boil. Cook for about 5 to 7 minutes, stirring frequently. Remove the syrup mixture from the heat and add baking soda, maple whisky, chopped pecans and almonds. Pour the maple mixture over the popcorn and stir.

Stir the popcorn every 10 minutes or so while it is baking.

Temperature: 250°F (120°C)

Baking Time: 1 hour

Yield: about 12 cups (3 L)

Maple Syrup Fudge Sauce

Here is another recipe developed by Jeremy Stevens of the Great Canadian Fudge Company. Jeremy adapted this recipe especially for Maple Moon™ readers so that they could make it on a limited basis. If you aren't a manufacturer, it's probably just as well to avoid having vats of this good stuff sitting around. See the description of their company on page 110.

2¼ cups	water	530 mL
	pinch of salt	
⅔ cup	clear corn syrup	150 mL
⅞ cup	white sugar	205 mL
1 tbsp.	butter	15 mL
2½ cups	condensed milk (2 cans)	600 mL
⅔ cup	hot water	150 mL
4 tbsp.	pure maple syrup	60 mL

Place the water and salt in a large, stainless steel saucepan over medium heat. Add corn syrup and sugar. Stir constantly with a wooden spoon, making sure to scrape down any excess sugar that clings to the side of the pan. If the sides of the pot aren't cleared of sugar, the sauce could end up grainy. Dissolve all of the sugar and then turn the heat down and add the butter to the sugar mixture. Stir in. Remove from heat and stir in the condensed milk. Stir well. Place the sauce back on the element and stir constantly. DO NOT STOP. Turn the heat back to medium. After a few minutes, the sauce will start a full, rolling boil. STIR CONSTANTLY so that the sauce won't stick and burn. Boil for 7 to 10 minutes, then add ⅔ cup (150 mL) of hot water and keep on medium heat for another 5 minutes. Remove from heat and stir in maple syrup. Pour into a container with a tight lid, e.g., a 1-quart (1 L) sealer with a screw top, and place in the refrigerator. Cool for 12 hours, so the sauce can thicken. Stir prior to using.

Preparation Time: 30 minutes

Yield: 1 quart (1 L)

This sauce is great for ice cream, pancakes, waffles or straight out of the bowl. It can be frozen and defrosted. Jeremy advises heating up some sauce in a microwave and then pouring it over pancakes!

Maple Cappuccino Mousse

This is a spectacular dessert and, contrary to the belief of some, it isn't one bit sinful.

¼ cup	cold water	60 mL
1	envelope unflavoured gelatin (¼ oz./7 g)	1
2 tbsp.	instant coffee	30 mL
2 cups	whipping cream	500 mL
2	eggs	2
½ cup	maple sugar	125 mL
3 tbsp.	Dutch cocoa	45 mL
¼ cup	maple cream liqueur	60 mL
1 tsp.	cinnamon	5 mL
1 tbsp.	maple sugar	15 mL
1 tsp.	cinnamon	5 mL
1 cup	whipping cream	250 mL
3 tbsp.	maple sugar	45 mL
6	cinnamon sticks (optional)	6

Place the water in a small saucepan and, over low heat, slowly dissolve the gelatin. Add the instant coffee granules and stir constantly to dissolve. Place whipping cream, eggs, ½ cup (125 mL) maple sugar, Dutch cocoa, maple cream liqueur and cinnamon in a blender and process. Add the gelatin mixture and process again, making sure that all ingredients are completely incorporated. Pour the mousse mixture into 4 to 6 crystal highball glasses or similar lovely glass serving dishes with high sides. Chill.

Combine the maple sugar and cinnamon in a small mixing bowl. Set aside. Whip the cream with 3 tbsp. (45 mL) maple sugar until stiff. Garnish the mousse with dollops of whipped cream or place the whipped cream into a pastry bag with a decorative tip and use your imagination. Sprinkle each serving with the cinnamon/maple sugar mixture. Garnish with cinnamon sticks for an impressive presentation.

Serves: 4 to 6, depending on appetites

Maple Custard

This Maple Custard is sublime. Creamy, smooth and rich, it is a simple yet sumptuous dessert.

¾ cup	maple syrup	175 mL
4	eggs	4
2 cups	half and half cream	500 mL
1 tsp.	maple cream liqueur	5 mL

Add the syrup to the eggs and beat well. Beat in the cream and maple cream liqueur. Spoon into 5 or 6 custard cups.

Place custard cups into a baking pan that has been filled with water to come up the sides of the custard cups about 1½" (4 cm).

Temperature: 350°F (180°C)

Baking Time: 35 to 45 minutes

Serve custard warm or cool. Custard may be refrigerated for several hours or overnight.

Variation: To make **Maple Crème Brûlée**, sprinkle about 2 tsp. (10 mL), ⅛" (3 mm) of maple sugar over each well-chilled custard. Set the custard cups on a baking sheet.

Preheat the broiler. Broil the custard just until the sugar melts and forms a crust. Many chefs use a blowtorch to caramelize the sugar – holding the flame 2" (5 cm) above the sugar, until it melts and forms a crust. Let the custard cool and then refrigerate it until you are ready to serve it.

Maple Rice Pudding

If you have unused rice sitting around, this is a great solution for leftovers. Alternatively, it's also great if you just plain love rice pudding.

1	envelope unflavoured gelatin (¼ oz./7 g)	1
¼ cup	cold water	60 mL
1½ cups	half and half cream	375 mL
⅓ cup	maple sugar	75 mL
2	eggs, slightly beaten	2
1 tbsp.	maple syrup liqueur	15 mL
1 tsp.	cinnamon	5 mL
2 cups	cooked white rice	500 mL
1 cup	dark raisins	250 mL
½ cup	maple sugar	125 mL

In a large saucepan, sprinkle unflavoured gelatin over water and stir for about 1 minute. Turn heat on low and stir for another 3 to 4 minutes, until the gelatin is completely dissolved. Add half and half cream and maple sugar and stir constantly. Remove from heat and add eggs, maple syrup liqueur and cinnamon.

Pour the custard mixture into a large bowl and chill for about an hour. Add the rice and raisins. Chill in the refrigerator for about another 3 hours.

Serve sprinkled with maple sugar.

Serves: 6 (or 3 teenagers)

Maple Raisin Bread Pudding

Leftover bread can be annoying if you always have your mama's voice in your head about waste and starvation. In New Orleans they know how to make the most of their leftover bread. It seems like every restaurant features Bread Pudding with a fabulous Whisky, Rum or Brandy Sauce. Here is a great solution for dessert, breakfast or a snack.

5 cups	stale bread, crusty French bread is best	1.25 L
4	eggs	4
3 cups	half and half cream	750 mL
½ cup	maple syrup	125 mL
⅓ cup	sugar	75 mL
1 tsp.	cinnamon	5 mL
1 tsp.	salt	5 mL
1 tbsp.	maple syrup liqueur	15 mL
1½ cups	dark raisins	375 mL
½ cup	slivered almonds (optional)	125 mL

Place all of the crumbled bread in a greased and floured 9 x 13" (23 x 33 cm) baking pan. Combine the remaining ingredients, except the almonds, in a large bowl and pour over the stale bread. Sprinkle the almonds over last. Bake on the middle rack. Serve with fresh berries from your garden.

Temperature: 350°F (180°C)

Baking Time: 40 minutes on the middle rack

Serves: 6

Maple Whisky Sauce

This sauce adds a luxurious note to bread puddings.

½ cup	maple syrup	125 mL
¾ cup	sugar	175 mL
1 cup	butter	250 mL
2	eggs, beaten until foamy	2
¾ cup	maple whisky OR maple cream liqueur	175 mL

In a small heavy saucepan, bring the syrup, sugar and butter just to a boil; stir to dissolve the sugar. Remove from heat and let cool slightly. Whisk in eggs and then the whisky. Serve warm over bread pudding.

Maple
Pies

Baking and Cooking with Maple Sugar and Maple Syrup

Many of the recipes in this book call for the use of maple sugar in place of white sugar. Maple sugar imparts a lovely flavour to recipes. The flavour differs markedly from recipes prepared with white sugar. If maple sugar is difficult to obtain, one solution is to prepare your own maple sugar, or you can purchase it in many specialty stores. Most gourmet stores in large urban centres carry maple sugar. Alternatively, you can access any of the corporations listed in the back of this book by e-mail, fax, phone or on their web sites. A Resource Section, see page 165, has been added for your convenience. These companies do business worldwide and will ship on demand.

If you want to prepare your own soft maple sugar, the first order of business is to clear all small children out of the kitchen and keep them out until you are absolutely finished. Begin by boiling maple syrup to 227°F (110°C). Then cool it to 160°F (71°C). Stir constantly for 15 to 20 minutes, until crystals begin to form. This type of sugar is called "Indian sugar" as it was the granulated type that was preferred by the indigenous people.

Helen and Scott Nearing discuss their method of preparation in *The Maple Sugar Book*:

> *Raise the temperature (of the maple syrup) as high as you dare without scorching. The syrup seems to boil almost dry and becomes high in the kettle and almost explosive. A thermometer is of little use as the bottom of the pan must be continuously scraped to prevent scorching. After taken [sic] from the fire, as soon as the syrup has subsided in the pan, the batch is beaten briskly for many minutes (ten or fifteen), when it thickens considerably and finally forms in small and separate grains.*

For the faint of heart, it's probably a better idea to purchase the sugar from the experts. Still, when you purchase ready-made products, a lot is lost. There is so much satisfaction in making your own products.

In the Sugaring-Off Festivals throughout the Maritimes, Québec, Ontario and Vermont, a highlight for children is the creation of "sugar on snow" or "maple wax". The trick is to ascertain when the maple syrup is ready. C.T. Alvord, an American writing in *Agricultural Report* in 1880, had this to say:

> *There are various ways of telling when the sugar is boiled enough. A convenient and good way is, when snow can be obtained, to have a dish of snow, and when some of the hot sugar is put on the snow, if it does not run into the snow, but cools in the form of wax on the surface of the snow, it is done enough to be put into tubs to drain. But when it is to be caked or stirred, it should be boiled until, when it is cooled on the snow, it will break like ice or glass.*

Cooking and baking with maple syrup is easy once you get used to it, but you do have to be mindful of a few rules. Maple syrup is a sweetener just like cane sugar, but a volume adjustment is necessary. To replace a cup (250 mL) of white sugar in any recipe, increase the sweetening by 50 percent. That is, 1½ cups (375 mL) of maple syrup for every 1 cup (250 mL) of white sugar in the recipe, and decrease any liquid measurement, such as melted butter or milk, by 2 tablespoons (30 mL) for every 1 cup (250 mL) volume of the liquid.

You will also notice that when you cook or bake with maple syrup, there is a tendency towards carmelization. Instead of having a golden pie crust, ugly little burned edges will appear and destroy your reputation. The trick is to reduce oven temperatures by 25°F (15°C) and check often toward the end of the baking process. As with everything else in life, you will get better with practice. Just remember that the indigenous people who used maple syrup and maple sugar prepared all of their meals using stone tools, birch bark containers and hollowed-out logs.

You will note throughout this book that there is little use of vanilla extract. It is traditional in North America to use vanilla extract for most baking recipes. I made the decision to use maple cream liqueur, Canadian maple whisky and maple syrup liqueur throughout the book because that's what I've been doing since I became aware of these excellent products. The recipes were tested using only these products, with excellent results. Maple cream liqueur, maple whisky and maple syrup liqueur can be obtained in major centres at liquor stores. Their trade names and access information are listed in the Resource Section at the back of this book.

There will be those who argue that maple syrup is much more expensive than white sugar, consequently, making the end cost of the recipe dramatically higher. My response is that maple syrup is organic and so is much healthier for us than white sugar, therefore the cost is worth it. The historical position of the settlers, as well as the indigenous people, was that maple syrup was a great homeopathic remedy for rheumatism (arthritis). Keep in mind that you aren't going to use gallons of maple syrup every day. Just a little in a recipe goes a long way to adding flavour, excitement and pizzazz.

Whatever you use to cook or bake, I suggest that all North Americans should experience a Sugaring-Off Festival at least once in their lives, and enjoy all of the treats that are available. In Ontario, the towns of Elmvale and Elmira host huge festivals, as do many other locales in this magnificent province. In Québec, visit the Beauce Maple Festival at Saint-Georges. In the Maritime Provinces and the State of Vermont, visitors and residents alike enjoy maple suppers and a festival spirit that dates back hundreds and hundreds of years. It's a once-in-a-lifetime experience.

Maple Butter Tarts

Butter tarts are a Canadian invention. These tarts combine two lovely Canadian traditions – maple syrup and butter tarts.

	pastry for 12 tart shells	
½ cup	unsalted butter	125 mL
2	eggs	2
¾ cup	maple syrup	175 mL
1 cup	raisins	250 mL
1 cup	pecans	250 mL
1 tsp.	salt	5 mL
1 tbsp.	maple syrup liqueur	15 mL

Place pastry into 12 large tart or cupcake pans. If you have purchased pre-made tart shells, that's just fine. Mix all filling ingredients together and pour into tart shells.

Preheat oven to 450°F (230°C). Bake tarts for 10 minutes at 450°F (230°C). Reduce heat to 425°F (220°C) and bake for another 10 minutes. Place tarts on the lowest rack in the oven to ensure that the crust is baked through. Watch carefully so they don't burn.

Yield: 12 large tarts

Never-Fail Pie Crust

My friends say they can't make good pie pastry. As with everything else, making pastry just takes practise and a willingness to experiment.

6 cups	all-purpose flour	1.5 L
1 tsp.	salt	5 mL
2 cups	lard	500 mL
2 tbsp.	vinegar	30 mL
2	eggs	2
¾ cup	ice water	175 mL

Mix flour and salt together and then cut in lard until crumbly. Mix the vinegar, eggs and water and add to the flour mixture. Mix well with your hands. Divide dough into 6 portions and form into balls.

Place a generous amount of flour on the kitchen counter and place a dough ball on the flour. Sprinkle the top of the ball liberally with flour and roll the dough out with a rolling pin.

Yield: 6 pie shells for 9" (23 cm) pies

aple Syrup Pie

The recipes for this traditional Québec treat vary immensely. Each is a little different and very, very rich.

	pastry for a 9" (23 cm) pie (see recipe on page 124)	
1 cup	maple syrup	250 mL
⅓ cup	cake/pastry flour	75 mL
½ cup	water at room temperature	125 mL
4	egg yolks, beaten	4
4 tbsp.	unsalted butter	60 mL
1 tbsp.	maple syrup liqueur	15 mL

Prepare the pastry.

To make the filling, pour the maple syrup into a saucepan and heat. Add the cake flour to the water in a plastic container. Cover and shake well to dissolve the flour. Stir into the maple syrup. Stir in beaten egg yolks and cook for about 7 minutes. Always use low to medium heat. Add the butter and melt. Add the maple syrup liqueur.

Pour the filling into the pie shell.

Temperature: 350°F (180°C)

Baking Time: 45 minutes. Watch carefully so that the pie doesn't burn.

Top with Maple Meringue Topping, see below.

Serves: 8

aple Meringue Topping

This is the icing on the cake – oh, you know what I mean!

6	egg whites at room temperature	6
1 tsp.	cream of tartar	5 mL
3 tbsp.	maple syrup	45 mL

Beat the egg whites until foamy. Add the cream of tartar and continue to beat until egg whites are stiff. Add the maple syrup slowly and continue beating until peaks are stiff and shiny.

Place the meringue on top of the baked Maple Syrup Pie and increase oven heat to 375°F (190°C). Bake until the top of the meringue is golden in colour. Remove immediately and serve.

Maple Sugar Pie
Tarte au Sucre

Sweet, rich and "fudgy", Tarte au Sucre is a very old Québec recipe with many variations. Maple sugar was used in the oldest versions, but today many recipes call for half maple sugar and half brown sugar or even (horrors!) all brown sugar. Serve small portions with whipped cream or ice cream.

	pastry for an 8" (20 cm) single-crust pie (see recipe on page 124)	
2 cups	maple sugar OR 1 cup (250 mL) EACH maple and brown sugar	500 mL
2 tbsp.	flour OR cornstarch	30 mL
1 cup	whipping cream	250 mL

Prepare the pastry and line the pie plate with it. Combine the sugar(s) and flour. Stir in the cream. Pour the filling into the prepared pie shell.

Temperature: 400°F (200°C)

Baking Time: 35 to 40 minutes, until filling is golden brown. Watch carefully.

Serve warm, but let stand for about 1 hour before serving.

Variations: Line small tart pans with pastry, fill and bake for **Maple Sugar Tarts**. Reduce baking time to 20 to 25 minutes. Watch carefully.

Some versions of this pie add a top crust. Seal, cut in steam vents, brush with cream and sprinkle with 2 to 3 tbsp. (30 to 45 mL) of maple sugar before baking.

Serves: 8

Québec Maple Sugar Pie

As Canada's largest maple syrup producer, Québec deserves to have this delicious pie named after "la belle province". Truly a taste of spring, this pie is a provincial tradition, each family has its own variation and they're all delicious.

	9" (23 cm) single pie crust (see page 124)	
1 cup	brown sugar	250 mL
1 cup	maple sugar	250 mL
1 cup	whipping cream	250 mL
1 cup	chopped pecans	250 mL
1 tbsp.	maple whisky OR maple cream liqueur	15 mL

Québec Maple Sugar Pie
(continued)

Prepare the pastry and line the pie plate with it. Mix brown sugar, maple sugar and cream in a saucepan. Bring to a boil over very low heat, being extremely careful not to scorch it. Cook for about 10 minutes and then remove from heat. Stir in pecans. Cool the filling for about an hour and then pour into the pie shell.

Temperature: 375°F (190°C)

Baking Time: 35 minutes on middle oven rack

Cool and serve with Maple Whipped Cream, see pages 19. 28 or 141.

Serves: 8

Blueberry Pie

I like big pies. To my way of thinking, a pie has to be like a Saskatchewan sky at sunset. Big!! The cheesy little servings with the instant fillings that you get at a lot of restaurants just aren't worth showing up for. Wild or tame, blueberries are heavenly in pies. Adding maple sugar may be gilding the lily – but you're worth it!

	pastry for a 10" (25 cm) 2-crust pie	
1 cup	maple sugar	250 mL
4 tbsp.	tapioca flour	60 mL
1 tsp.	cinnamon	5 mL
6 cups	fresh blueberries	1.5 L
1 tbsp.	butter	15 mL
2 tbsp.	lemon juice	30 mL

Prepare the pastry according to the recipe on page 124. Line the pie plate with the pastry.

Combine sugar, flour and cinnamon. Pour the blueberries into the pie shell.

Pour the maple sugar mixture over the blueberries. Dot with butter and sprinkle with lemon juice. Roll out the top crust and place over the blueberries. Pinch the edges of the pie to seal and cut off any excess dough. Cut vents for steam to escape. Brush the top crust with cream or milk. Sprinkle with maple sugar or white sugar. Place the pie on a foil-lined baking sheet to save oven cleanups.

Temperature: 350°F (180°C)

Baking Time: 1 hour and 10 minutes

Serves: 8

Apple Blueberry Pie with Maple Sugar Crust

The apple was introduced to North America by the Pilgrims at Plymouth Rock around 1620. The native Wampanoags gave the Pilgrims tobacco, corn, cranberries and native berries. When two cultures meet, the common ground is seldom language; the best meeting place is always food and music. This recipe is a tribute to that long-ago fusion of cultures.

Maple Sugar Crust:

2 cups	all-purpose flour	500 mL
¾ cup	yellow cornmeal	175 mL
5 tbsp.	maple sugar	75 mL
1½ tsp.	cinnamon	7 mL
1 tsp.	salt	5 mL
¾ cup	vegetable shortening	175 mL
3 tbsp.	buttermilk	45 mL
3 tbsp.	cream	45 mL
1 cup	fresh blueberries	250 mL
1½ cups	maple sugar	375 mL
2 tsp.	cinnamon	10 mL
6 cups	peeled, sliced Granny Smith apples	1.5 L
½ cup	dark raisins	125 mL
⅓ cup	all-purpose flour	75 mL
	whole milk OR cream	
	maple sugar OR white sugar	

To make the crust, mix the first 5 ingredients in a bowl and then cut in vegetable shortening until mixture resembles oatmeal. Add buttermilk and cream and work (but do NOT overwork) into a dough ball. Divide dough in 2 and wrap in waxed paper. Let the dough rest for an hour or so before rolling it out for the pie.

Apple Blueberry Pie with Maple Sugar Crust

(continued)

Place half of the dough on a well-floured counter and roll out with a rolling pin until it is a thickness that you find satisfactory. If you are inexperienced at this, you must keep trying until you get it right, or import your grandma to help out. Place the dough in a 10" (25 cm) pie plate.

Combine all of the remaining ingredients, except the milk and sugar, in a large bowl and pour into the pie shell. Roll out the top crust and place over the fruit. Pinch the edges of the pie crusts to seal; cut off any excess dough. Cut vents for steam to escape.

Roll out remaining dough and cut out maple leaf shapes. Using a pastry brush, paint the leaves on the top and bottom with milk. Sprinkle leaves with sugar and bake. It is the milk that gives the pie crust a lovely golden colour.

Place the pie on a baking sheet to protect your oven if it bubbles over. Bake in the lowest third of a preheated oven.

Temperature: 350°F (180°C)

Baking Time: 1 hour, 25 minutes

Note: Avoid burning pie by baking, uncovered, for 40 minutes. Then, cover the pie loosely with aluminum foil and bake for another 20 to 25 minutes.

Maple Peach Pie

Farm women at country fairs always compete for excellence in pies. This is the kind you'd find at a country fair in British Columbia, Ontario, Vermont or Maine.

	pastry for a 9" (23 cm) single-crust pie	
5 cups	sliced, peeled, fresh peaches	1.25 L
¾ cup	maple syrup	175 mL
2 tsp.	cinnamon	10 mL
3 tbsp.	tapioca flour	45 mL
1⅓ cups	yogurt	325 mL
½ cup	dark brown sugar	125 mL
¼ cup	maple cream liqueur	60 mL
½ cup	chopped hazelnuts OR macadamia nuts	125 mL

Prepare pastry according to the recipe on page 124. Place the pastry in the pie plate.

Arrange the drained peach slices in the pie shell. Mix maple syrup, cinnamon, tapioca flour and yogurt until completely incorporated. Pour over the peaches and bake.

Keep a careful eye on the pie as maple syrup has a tendency to caramelize.

Temperature: 425°F (220°C), lower to 325°F (160°C)

Baking Time: 15 minutes at 425°F (220°C); then 35 minutes at 325°F (160°C)

Sprinkle brown sugar over the pie and then drizzle on the maple cream liqueur. Return the pie to the warm oven for 5 minutes (with the door open) and melt the sugar. Sprinkle with nuts.

Allow the pie to cool and serve in about an hour.

Serves: 8

Variation: For a **Maple Peach Blueberry Pie**, sprinkle 1 cup (250 mL) of fresh blueberries over the peach filling before baking.

Pictured on page 139.

Maple Moon Rhubarb Pie

Just as the sap starts to run in the trees, another more subtle subterranean miracle begins to happen right across the Northern Hemisphere. As the ground begins to thaw, little strawberry-coloured spears start to poke through the ground. After a few weeks, it's rhubarb harvest time. It's a good idea to make pies out of the first strawberry rhubarb because it never seems as sweet later in the summer.

This big pie will go quickly as everyone loves the first fruit from the garden.

	pastry for a 10" (25 cm) 2-crust pie (see recipe on page 124)	
6-7 cups	chopped rhubarb	1.5-1.75 L
2 cups	maple sugar	500 mL
2 tbsp.	flour	30 mL
2	eggs	2
1 tbsp.	lemon zest	15 mL
1 tbsp.	lemon juice	15 mL
2 tbsp.	half and half cream	30 mL
3 tbsp.	white sugar OR maple sugar	45 mL

Line the pie plate with the pastry.

Mix the rhubarb in a large bowl with the syrup, tapioca, eggs, lemon zest and lemon juice. Pour the filling into the pie shell and place the upper crust on top. Seal and flute the edges and cut vents for steam to escape. Brush the top of the pie crust with half and half cream. Sprinkle sugar on the pie crust. For an interesting variation, sprinkle maple sugar on the top of the crust.

Temperature: 350°F (180°C)

Baking Time: 1 hour, 10 minutes

Deep Dutch Maple Apple Pie

The Dutch national treat is "appeltaart". There are close to one million immigrants of direct Dutch and mixed Dutch descent in Canada. The Dutch adore all things sweet and Canadian history books show that the Dutch were involved at a very early stage with the maple sap harvest. This recipe is a fusion of the magic of two cultures.

Sweet Dough:

3 cups	all-purpose flour	750 mL
1 cup	white sugar	250 mL
⅓ cup	maple sugar	75 mL
1 cup	unsalted butter	250 mL
2	eggs	2

Maple Apple Filling:

6-8	Granny Smith apples, peeled and chopped	6-8
1 cup	raisins	250 mL
1	lemon, grated zest of	1
1½ cups	maple sugar	375 mL
1 tsp.	cinnamon	5 mL

Topping:

2 cups	whipping cream	500 mL
½ cup	icing sugar	125 mL
	maple syrup	

To make the dough, combine flour and sugars. Cut butter into small pieces and add to flour. Add 1 beaten egg and mix with your hands until smooth and uniformly coloured. Refrigerate the dough while you prepare the filling.

To prepare the filling, combine apples and all of the remaining filling ingredients. Line a 10" (25 cm), greased springform pan with part of the refrigerated dough, ⅛" (.3 cm) thick on the bottom and a little thicker on the sides. Place the filling in the pastry shell. Roll out the remaining dough and cut it into strips to create a lattice-work top for the tart. Brush the lattice work with the remaining beaten egg.

Temperature: 350°F (180°C)

Baking Time: 1¼ hours

 132

Deep Dutch Maple Apple Pie

(continued)

Whip the cream with the icing sugar and serve the tart with dollops of whipped cream and a drizzle of maple syrup.

Note: Be sure that you make the bottom dough a little thinner. This is such a deep tart that there may be problems with an uncooked bottom shell. To avoid this, bake the tart on the very bottom rack of the oven.

Maple Apple Crisp Pie

This crunchy topping is perfect with apples, and it is even better with the addition of maple sugar.

	pastry for a 10" (25 cm) single crust pie	
	pastry for a 10" (25 cm) single crust pie	
1 tbsp.	flour	15 mL
6 cups	sliced Granny Smith apples	1.5 L
1 tbsp.	tapioca flour	15 mL
2	eggs	2
1½ cups	maple sugar OR syrup	375 mL
2 tsp.	cinnamon	10 mL
½ tsp.	nutmeg	2 mL
1 tbsp.	butter	15 mL
1 tbsp.	lemon juice	15 mL

Oatmeal Maple Sugar Topping:

1 cup	rolled oats	250 mL
½ cup	maple sugar	125 mL
⅓ cup	all-purpose flour	75 mL
⅓ cup	unsalted butter	75 mL

Place the pastry in the pie plate and sprinkle the uncooked pie crust with 1 tbsp. (15 mL) of flour. Arrange the apples in the pie shell. Mix tapioca flour, eggs, maple sugar, spices and butter. Spoon over the apples and sprinkle with lemon juice.

For the topping, combine rolled oats, maple sugar, flour and butter. Sprinkle over the apples and bake.

Temperature: 350°F (180°C)

Baking Time: 1 hour

Maple Raisin Pie

During the long winters in the more northerly sections of North America, it was very difficult in the days before long-haul trucking and flight to obtain fruit. Throughout the early pioneer years, the women settlers had their work cut out for them in keeping up the vitamin levels of their large families. These women developed this delicious pie.

	pastry for a 9" (23 cm) 2-crust pie (see recipe on page 124)	
3 cups	seedless, dark raisins	750 mL
3 cups	hot water	750 mL
1 cup	maple syrup	250 mL
3 tbsp.	cornstarch	45 mL
1 tbsp	maple syrup liqueur	15 mL
2 tbsp.	butter	30 mL
2 tbsp.	lemon juice	30 mL
1 tsp.	lemon zest	5 mL
2 tbsp.	half and half cream	30 mL
3 tbsp.	maple sugar*	45 mL

Prepare the pastry.

Combine the raisins and water in a large saucepan and simmer for 15 minutes. Combine maple syrup and cornstarch and add to the raisins. Cook until thick and remove from the heat. Stir in maple syrup liqueur, butter, lemon juice and lemon zest. Cool the filling and then pour into the pie shell.

Cover the pie with the upper crust and seal pastry edges. Cut vents for steam to escape. Paint the cream on the top crust with a pastry brush and sprinkle liberally with the maple sugar.

Temperature: 425°F (220°C), lower to 350°F (180°C)

Baking Time: 15 minutes at 425°F (220°C); then 35 to 40 minutes at 350°F (180°C)

* ALWAYS paint your pie crust with whole milk or cream and then sprinkle with sugar or with maple sugar. There is nothing worse than an anaemic-looking pie that shows up at a bake sale and then sits there because the cook was too cheap to make it look presentable.

Maple

Cakes,
Squares
&
Cookies

Sugaring Off

Anxious to witness the awesome beauty of the magnificent rock or sugar maple, and harvest its incredible nectar, Europeans moved these small trees to their various countries and tried to cultivate them. The transplanting was relatively futile as they lacked the essential ingredient required by all sugar bushes: temperature gradation. When the temperature dips below freezing at nights, and the sun is warm during the day, the sap starts to run. Consequently, sugaring off became impossible. In 1892, American Charles Sprague Sargent wrote of the maple in Europe,

> The sugar Maple, like the Hickories, the White Oaks and other upland trees of Eastern America, does not flourish in the Old World, and really fine specimens, if they exist at all in Europe, are extremely rare, although 150 years have passed since it was introduced, and at different times, considerable attention has been given to its cultivation.

Ontario, Québec, part of the Maritimes in Canada, and the New England States are those lucky areas where people go in the tens of thousands to Sugaring-Off Festivals. They shrug off the confinement of long dark nights and deep banks of snow and embrace the coming spring with a passion. The rising of the sap in the maple tree is a heady metaphor for renewal or rebirth for the inhabitants of these blessed provinces and states.

The province of Québec produces 85% of Canada's maple syrup. Entire extended families go to the four-hundred-odd sugar shacks and feast on maple syrup cooked with beans, maple-cured hams, crêpes covered with maple syrup and the famous Québecois *oreilles de crisse* or the "ears of Christ", strips of salt pork or bacon cooked in maple syrup. The ultimate treat is saved for last. Fresh maple syrup is poured on pristine snow and the resulting taffy is eagerly consumed. Children varying in ages from 1 to 104, delight in this treat, and family lore is filled with seasonal memories. In Ontario, the Maritimes, particularly New Brunswick, and the New England states, the scene is no different. Everyone knows that everything is better with maple syrup.

The sugar shack was the scene of the sugaring off as the 97% of the water content was boiled off over fires fed by maple wood. Seasoned harvesters reported that their eyelashes would stick together from the sugar-filled atmosphere, not altogether a negative working condition if you have a good, hot shower at the end of a tiring day. In years past, horses hauled the thousands of buckets of sap collected at the tap sites. Today, miles of plastic tubing connect the lovely trees as they are tapped. It takes about 40 gallons of maple sap and a lot of hard work to yield one gallon of maple syrup, so let's not hear any complaints from you city folk about the cost of this priceless product.

Maple Heaven Carrot Cake

Coffee shops today are the bars of the late twentieth and early twenty-first centuries. In Toronto, Seattle, Vancouver and many other cities, you see the famous café society of Paris being recreated. Students linger over their gourmet coffees, businessmen and women finalize deals, young people meet for an inexpensive date, mothers discuss their children's latest achievements. In short, you witness life and it is delightful.

Many of these shops sell carrot cake and it seems to disappear at an alarming rate, so let's not have a nonsensical discussion about calories. This recipe is worth the indulgence.

3 cups	maple syrup	750 mL
3 cups	cake/pastry flour	750 mL
3½ cups	shredded carrots*	825 mL
2 tsp.	baking soda	10 mL
1½ cups	vegetable oil	375 mL
4	large eggs at room temperature	4
1 tbsp.	lemon zest	15 mL
1 tbsp.	maple whisky	15 mL
1½ cups	raisins	375 mL
½ cup	pine nuts OR chopped hazelnuts	125 mL
1½ cups	whipping cream	375 mL
4 tbsp.	icing sugar OR maple sugar	60 mL

Mix the maple syrup and cake flour together in a large bowl. Add the shredded carrots, baking soda and oil. Beat in eggs, 1 at a time. Add the lemon zest, maple whisky, raisins and nuts. Mix thoroughly. Set the whipping cream and icing sugar aside. Pour the batter into a 9 x 13" (23 x 33 cm) cake pan that has been thoroughly greased and dusted with flour.

OR, for **Maple Carrot Muffins**, spray large muffin cups with non-stick spray.

Temperature: 350°F (180°C)

Baking Time: 30 to 35 minutes for the cake. Check for doneness (I stab the cake with a turkey skewer). Muffins will take 15 to 20 minutes, depending on the size that you choose to bake.

Whip cream with icing sugar until stiff. Serve cake with whipped cream.

Yield: 1 cake or 24 large muffins

* *Reduce carrots by ½ cup (125 mL) if you are using carrots fresh from the garden. Summer carrots have a much higher moisture content.*

137

Maple Pound Cake

Pound cake is a classic. It can be used as the base for a trifle, see page 103, or as an accompaniment to a fruit salad, see pages 90 to 92.

1 lb.	unsalted butter	500 g
2 cups	berry/superfine sugar	500 mL
1½ cups	maple syrup	375 mL
6	eggs	6
4 cups	flour	1 L
1 tbsp.	baking powder	15 mL
1 tsp.	baking soda	5 mL
1 tsp.	salt	5 mL
1 cup	whole milk	250 mL
1 tbsp.	maple cream liqueur OR maple syrup liqueur	15 mL

Cream the butter and sugar together in a large bowl. Beat until the mixture is light and fluffy. Add maple syrup and incorporate fully.

Add the eggs, 1 at a time, beating after each addition.

Sift the dry ingredients together and add the dry ingredients and the milk to the butter mixture in alternating additions. Add maple cream liqueur last and mix by hand. Do not beat excessively.

Pour the batter into 2 well-greased and floured 5 x 9" (13 x 23 cm) loaf pans.

Bake in a preheated oven.

Temperature: 350°F (180°C)

Baking Time: 1 hour

Maple Peach Pie, page 130

Maple Apple Cake

This cake smells great, tastes great and looks great. Make sure that you cover it with plastic wrap or ice it completely with icing or whipped cream, otherwise it will dry out quickly.

3 cups	cake/pastry flour	750 mL
1 tbsp.	cinnamon	15 mL
2 tsp.	baking soda	10 mL
1 cup	unsalted butter	250 mL
1 cup	maple syrup	250 mL
3	eggs	3
1 cup	hot strong coffee	250 mL
4	tart apples, peeled, cored and coarsely chopped	4
½ cup	pecans	125 mL
1 cup	raisins	250 mL
2 cups	whipping cream	500 mL
½ cup	icing sugar*	125 mL

Combine the flour, cinnamon and baking soda. Mix the butter and maple syrup in a separate bowl. Add eggs, 1 at a time, and then add half of the flour and half of the coffee. While continuing to mix, add the remaining flour and coffee. Stir in the chopped apple, pecans and raisins. Pour into a 9 x 13" (23 x 33 cm) cake pan and bake.

Temperature: 350°F (180°C)

Baking Time: 1 hour

Serves: 10 to 12

Whip the cream with the icing sugar and serve the cake with a dollop of whipped cream.

* For **Maple Whipped Cream**, *use maple sugar to sweeten the whipping cream, but you will have to cut the volume down because maple sugar is sweeter than white sugar. Cut by one-third for appropriate sweetness.*

Vermont Maple Fudge Cake, page 162

Maple Butter Icing, page 143

Chocolate Butterflies, page 149

Maple Syrup Cake

I use macadamia nuts in this recipe because I like the idea of the symbiosis of two fantastic trees. Both the maple tree and the macadamia tree are hardwoods. The macadamia nut is incredibly hard and extricating it from its shell is hard work. You practically have to use a bomb to get it out, which explains the price. Never mind that. Nothing worthwhile is accomplished without effort. I like to think that this recipe is a marriage of Hawaii and North America, at least in terms of trees and flavour.

1 cup	unsalted butter	250 mL
1¼ cups	maple syrup	300 mL
3	eggs	3
1 tbsp.	maple whisky	15 mL
1½ cups	cake/pastry flour	375 mL
1 tsp.	salt	5 mL
1 tsp.	baking powder	5 mL
2 tsp.	baking soda	10 mL
1 cup	chopped macadamia nuts OR hazelnuts	250 mL

Cream together the butter and maple syrup. Add the eggs, 1 at a time, and incorporate fully. Add maple whisky, flour, salt, baking powder and baking soda.

Pour the batter into 2 well-greased and floured layer pans. Divide nuts in half and sprinkle half over the batter in each pan.

Temperature: 350°F (180°C)

Baking Time: 20 to 25 minutes

To serve, place 1 layer on a serving plate and ice with Maple Butter Icing, see page 143. Top with the second layer and ice the top and sides.

Serves: 8

Maple Butter Icing

I won't use anything except butter for icing because that's the way my mama did it. She rarely buys anything at bake sales because she's such a food snob. She gets along well with my best friend from college, Frank, because he's a food snob as well. Mama says a lot of people use cheap ingredients. She can always taste the lard that some cooks use as an extender. I do notice that at bake sales my mama's submissions are ALWAYS the first out the door.

1½ cups	unsalted butter	375 mL
½ cup	maple syrup	125 mL
1	egg	1
1 tsp.	salt	5 mL
2-3 cups	icing sugar	500-750 mL
1 tsp.	maple cream liqueur	5 mL

Cream the butter and maple syrup together. Add the egg and beat thoroughly. Add the salt and icing sugar and continue beating. Beat in the maple cream liqueur.

Use this icing on any of the chocolate cake recipes on pages 162 to 164.

Yield: 2 cups (500 mL)

Variation: Add ½ cup (125 mL) of Dutch cocoa to make **Maple Chocolate Butter Icing**.

Pictured on page 140.

143

Boiled Maple Icing

This icing is perfect for the Vermont Maple Fudge Cake, page 162. Boiled icings have a satiny sheen and texture, and a lovely smooth spreading consistency. They can be swirled and mounded to create very decorative effects.

5	egg whites	5
½ tsp.	cream of tartar	2 mL
1 tsp.	maple syrup liqueur	5 mL
1⅓ cups	maple syrup	325 mL

Beat the egg whites and cream of tartar until soft, shiny peaks form. Add the maple cream liqueur and incorporate completely.

In a heavy saucepan, gently boil the maple syrup until it gets to the soft ball stage, 240°F (120°C). Use a candy thermometer hooked to the side of your pan for perfect results. Slowly add the hot syrup to the egg whites and beat constantly at high speed. Continue beating until the icing is of a spreading consistency.

Yield: 2 cups (500 mL)

Maple Pecan Squares

Terry and Keith Corbould operate a lovely bed and breakfast in Bella Coola, British Columbia, Canada. Terry is a French Canadian chef and the author of Wilderness Elegance, *a cookbook she compiled while serving over nine years as the Chef at Tweedsmuir Lodge. The recipe was given to her by a good friend. This particular treat was often served at afternoon tea. Terry liked serving it to overseas guests because of the maple syrup. She was delighted to be able to serve it to Lady Mountbatten of Burma and her husband, Lord John Brabourne. She also served it to Lord John Tweedsmuir when he stayed for the fiftieth anniversary of the park that bears his name. Tweedsmuir Park is one of the spectacular British Columbia parks that attract people from all over the globe.*

Brown Sugar Base:

2 cups	flour	500 mL
½ cup	brown sugar	125 mL
1 cup	unsalted butter	250 mL

Maple Pecan Filling:

⅔ cup	brown sugar	150 mL
1 cup	maple syrup	250 mL
2	beaten eggs	2
¼ cup	unsalted butter	60 mL
¼ tsp.	salt	1 mL
½ tsp.	vanilla	2 mL
2 tbsp.	flour	30 mL
⅔ cup	pecan halves	150 mL

Mix all of the base ingredients together and press firmly over the bottom of a 7 x 9" (18 x 23 cm) pan. Bake for 5 minutes at 350°F (180°C).

In a small heavy saucepan, combine the sugar and syrup and simmer for about 5 minutes. Cool slightly. Pour the syrup over the beaten eggs and stir well. Mix in the butter, salt, vanilla and flour and pour over the base. Place the pecan halves on top.

Temperature: 400°F (200°C), lower to 350°F (180°C)

Baking Time: 10 minutes at 400°F (200°C); then 20 minutes at 350°F (180°C)

Yield: 20 to 24 squares

Raisin Oatmeal Maple Cookies

These cookies are nutritious and a great add-on to a mid-morning latte. If you have trouble with dark edges on the cookies, simply lower the temperature 25°F (15°C) and add 2 minutes to your baking time. These cookies are soft, so cool them completely before serving.

1 cup	unsalted butter	250 mL
¾ cup	packed dark brown sugar	175 mL
¾ cup	maple syrup	175 mL
2	eggs	2
1 tbsp.	maple whisky	15 mL
1½ cups	rolled oats	375 mL
1 cup	sweetened coconut	250 mL
2 tsp.	baking powder	10 mL
½ tsp.	baking soda	2 mL
½ tsp	salt	2 mL
1½ cups	all-purpose flour	375 mL
2 cups	dark raisins	500 mL

Place the butter, brown sugar, maple syrup and eggs in a large bowl and cream with a hand mixer. Add maple whisky and rolled oats. Stir well and add the coconut, baking powder, baking soda, salt and flour. Mix well, then stir in raisins.

Drop the dough in large spoonfuls onto a cookie sheet that has been sprayed with non-stick spray.

Temperature: 325°F (160°C)

Baking Time: 12 to 15 minutes

Yield: 18 to 24 cookies, depending on size

Maple

&

Chocolate –
Twin Passions

Tempering Chocolate

Use only the finest chocolate for baking. If you are going to consume the calories, why not consume the best? Cheap chocolate is easily recognizable by its sandy, waxy taste. A recent article by a noted food writer indicated her preferences when she wrote that if she is buying a cake with icing or chocolate, she wants a food item that she can savour, not something with which to grease the bottom of her Toyota. I couldn't agree with her more. Here's how you temper (melt), really good chocolate:

Use a clean, grease-free double boiler.

Fill the bottom pan with enough water to create a full, rolling boil. Reduce the heat.

Cut Dutch or Belgian chocolate into small pieces.

Place the pieces of chocolate into the top half of the double boiler. NEVER allow any moisture to touch the chocolate. Even 1 droplet of water will alter the chocolate's texture. Stir the chocolate, using medium heat to keep the water warm. If the water starts to boil too much, lower the heat – you do not want any water to escape between the pans.

Melt all of the chocolate and remove it from the heat. Allow the chocolate to cool in the refrigerator until it is quite cool. It will thicken again but this doesn't matter.

Warm the water bath again and replace the top half of the double boiler. Warm the chocolate slowly and test with a thermometer. The tempered chocolate should be 89°F (32°C).

If you are dipping strawberries, cookies, cherries, etc. into the chocolate, leave the chocolate in the top section of the double boiler and leave the heat on very low. If you want to achieve the lowest possible heat, you can purchase little simmer mats with handles to place between the heat and the bottom pan. This will achieve a very gentle warmth.

Once you gain some courage and start to work with properly tempered chocolate, it is relatively easy to become a "chocolate artist". Just remember that, as it hardens, chocolate will assume the shape of any container into which it is placed.

Chocolate Leaves:

Prepare a baking sheet by lining it with baking parchment. Obtain a clean, small paintbrush and paint the underside of a sturdy leaf. Deep-veined leaves make the best "moulds". The salal leaves (obtainable from any florist) from the forest floors of British Columbia are superb. Build up layers of chocolate on the back side of the leaf by repeatedly painting on the layers with a small paintbrush. Allow the leaves to harden in the refrigerator. Just prior to serving, take the hardened leaves and remove the fresh leaves by gently lifting or peeling them from the chocolate leaves.

Chocolate Butterflies:

Spoon cooled chocolate into a pastry bag which has been fitted with a small writing tip. Draw butterfly outlines on a piece of baking parchment and pipe along the lines. Chill the butterflies for about 25 minutes. The chocolate will begin to harden.

Using sharp scissors, cut the butterflies and the parchment paper into individual units, one butterfly per piece of paper. Carefully bend each butterfly so that it looks like it is flying or landing on a flower. The wings will be in a semi-open position. Support the butterflies as they harden further by placing each butterfly between the cups of an inverted egg container. Allow the butterflies to harden in the refrigerator for another hour. Carefully peel the parchment paper away from the butterflies.

Use the butterflies and the leaves as beautiful garnishes on cakes or other desserts.

Pictured on page 140.

Chocolate Shells or Cups:

You can make chocolate shells by wrapping the outside of large scallop shells with aluminum foil. Make sure that the foil imitates the shell shape perfectly. Remove the foil and gently paint the foil shell with several layers of tempered chocolate. Cool in the refrigerator on a baking sheet lined with baking parchment. Remove the foil and fill the chocolate shells with mousse, strawberry cream, etc.

You can make chocolate cups by painting the inside of cupcake or muffin forms/liners and supporting them inside muffin tins as you paint on the chocolate layers. Let them cool and harden in the refrigerator. Remove the hardened forms from the pans and gently peel off the liners. You are left with a chocolate cup which you can fill with anything you desire.

149

Maple Chocolate Mousse

This mousse is superb. It takes about twenty minutes to prepare with guaranteed rave reviews. When people ask for the recipe, as they inevitably will, you can present this one or mumble something like, "it's a family secret, it's been in the family for six generations". Whichever approach you choose, everyone will love this mousse.

⅔ cup	dark Dutch chocolate, tempered*	150 mL
½ cup	maple syrup	125 mL
5	eggs, separated and at room temperature	5
⅔ cup	berry/superfine sugar	150 mL
1 tbsp.	maple syrup liqueur	15 mL

Melt the chocolate and syrup together in the top section of a double boiler. Allow it to cool.

In a separate bowl, beat egg yolks until thickened and light. Mix into the chocolate.

In another bowl, beat egg whites until stiff but still moist. Add sugar gradually and beat the eggs until shiny.

Fold the beaten egg whites into the chocolate/maple syrup mixture. Mix in the maple syrup liqueur. Spoon into glass serving dishes.

Serves: 6

* See the tempering information on page 148.

Note: For a mousse that is a little less sweet, reduce the sugar by ⅓ cup (75 mL).

Maple Macadamia Mousse

Our family is nuts about nuts. Any "exotic" nut disappears at an incredible rate. Combine that love with a passion for real maple syrup and a love of sweets and this rich creamy mousse is the result.

6	large eggs, separated and at room temperature	6
⅔ cup	maple syrup	150 mL
4	extra egg whites	4
1½ cups	heavy cream	375 mL
4 tbsp.	maple syrup liqueur	60 mL
½ cup	dark Dutch chocolate, melted	125 mL
1 tbsp.	unsalted butter	15 mL
1 cup	finely chopped macadamia nuts	250 mL

Beat the 6 egg yolks on high speed until they are thick and light in colour.

Place the maple syrup in a saucepan and bring to a boil. Cook over medium to high heat for about 5 minutes, Watch the syrup carefully.

Add the maple syrup to the egg yolks and beat thoroughly until smooth and well blended.

In a separate bowl, beat the egg whites until they are stiff.

In another bowl, beat the cream until stiff peaks form.

Temper* the chocolate in a double boiler; stir in the butter and set aside

Using a large bowl, pour in the maple syrup and egg yolk mixture. Gently fold in the egg whites, whipped cream and maple cream liqueur. Spoon the mousse into attractive serving dishes – I like glass because you can see the richness of the mousse. Drizzle chocolate over each serving and then sprinkle with the macadamia nuts.

Serves: 6 to 8

* See the tempering information on page 148.

Chocolate Maple Mousse Cheesecake

You will need to run a marathon to justify diving into this dessert, but you will remember this cheesecake forever.

Chocolate Maple Crust:

2 cups	finely ground chocolate wafer cookies	500 mL
2 tbsp.	maple syrup	30 mL
¼ cup	unsalted butter, melted	60 mL

Chocolate Maple Cream Filling:

2 x 8 oz.	cream cheese	2 x 250 g
½ cup	maple syrup	125 mL
2	large eggs	2
1 cup	dark Dutch OR Belgian chocolate, melted and cooled*	250 mL
½ cup	maple cream liqueur OR maple syrup liqueur**	125 mL
⅔ cup	sour cream	150 mL

Topping:

1 cup	whipping cream, whipped stiff	250 mL
4 tbsp.	icing sugar	60 mL
12	Dutch OR Belgian chocolate wafers	12

To make the base, combine chocolate wafer crumbs, maple syrup and the melted butter; mix until completely integrated. Press crumb mixture into the bottom and sides of a buttered 8" (20 cm) springform pan (with removeable sides and bottom). Refrigerate until needed.

To make the filling, beat the cream cheese until smooth. Add the maple syrup slowly and beat until smooth. Add eggs 1 at a time, and beat until fluffy. Add the cooled chocolate, maple cream liqueur and sour cream. Blend completely and pour into the chilled chocolate maple crust.

Temperature: 300°F (150°C)

Baking Time: 1 hour

Chocolate Maple Mousse Cheesecake
(continued)

Remove the cheesecake from the oven and let it cool on the counter. Refrigerate overnight to set. You can serve this cheesecake within 4 hours or so of baking but, if you can keep it out of the hands of your family, it is easier to serve when it has set completely.

Make the topping just prior to serving. Whip the cream and icing sugar until stiff peaks form.

Remove the cheesecake from the springform pan and set it on a serving plate. You can cover the entire cheesecake (including the sides) with the whipped cream or you can leave the crumb sides exposed. It's your choice. Just make sure that you use a lot of whipped cream on the top because if you are going off your diet, you might as well go for broke. (You can use a pastry bag and pipe the whipped cream onto the top in a decorative manner, but only if you are creative, or have taken a cake decorating course, or if you've just won the lottery and have tons of time.)

Garnish with the 12 chocolate wafers and serve. To cut the cheesecake, you will have to use a large, sharp knife. It helps to dip the knife into hot water before you cut this masterpiece.

Serves 8 to 10.

*To melt chocolate, place chocolate in the top of a double boiler over medium heat. Slowly allow the steam to heat the chocolate. NEVER do this on high heat. You will scorch your Dutch chocolate and that's just too awful to think about. See the tempering notes on page 148.

**There are some very good maple "booze" products on the market. Some are maple syrup mixed with whisky and some are cream-based. All are very good. Please see the Resource Section on pages 165, 166 for product information.

Maple Chocolate Mousse Pie

If you like maple syrup a lot, and you like chocolate even more, this pie will make you very, very happy.

2 tbsp.	unsalted butter	30 mL
4 tbsp.	maple sugar	60 mL
1½ cups	coarsely chopped semisweet Dutch OR Belgian chocolate	375 mL
10	eggs, separated	10
½ cup	maple syrup	125 mL
3 tbsp.	maple cream liqueur	45 mL
2 cups	whipping cream	500 mL
⅓ cup	maple sugar	75 mL
6-8	chocolate-dipped strawberries	6-8

Use an oversized, 13" (33 cm) pie plate which has been well greased with unsalted butter. Sprinkle maple sugar all over the bottom of the greased pie plate.

Temper the Dutch chocolate in the top section of a double boiler. See tempering instructions on page 148. Set aside the melted chocolate and allow it to cool.

In a separate bowl, beat 10 egg yolks until they are light in colour. Gradually beat in the maple syrup until completely incorporated. Beat in the cooled chocolate and maple cream liqueur.

Beat the egg whites until stiff peaks form. Fold into the chocolate mixture until completely mixed. Measure 6 cups (1.5 L) of filling into the pie plate. This mixture will need to be cooked. Reserve the remaining chocolate mixture.

Temperature: 325°F (160°C)

Baking Time: 30 minutes

Cool the chocolate shell for about 1 hour. Place the remaining chocolate into the cooled shell and chill.

Whip the cream with the maple sugar until the cream is very stiff. Serve the pie topped with huge dollops of whipped cream and garnished with chocolate-coated strawberries.

You can also place whipped cream in a pastry bag and use a star tip to decorate the pie in an artistic fashion. For those in a hurry – skip this step.

Maple Pecan Chocolate Pie

Maple and chocolate make a great pie even better.

	pastry for a 9" (23 cm) single-crust pie (see recipe on page 124)	
¾ cup	chunks Dutch semisweet chocolate	175 mL
4 tbsp.	unsalted butter	60 mL
1 tbsp.	instant coffee	15 mL
⅓ cup	brown sugar	75 mL
1 cup	maple syrup	250 mL
4	eggs at room temperature, beaten	4
1 tbsp.	maple whisky	15 mL
1½ cups	pecan halves	375 mL

Prepare the pastry and line the pie plate. Temper the chocolate in the top section of a double boiler, see page 148, and add the butter 1 tbsp. (15 mL) at a time. Melt completely. Dissolve the instant coffee in the chocolate and butter. Stir until completely incorporated.

In a medium-sized saucepan, bring brown sugar and maple syrup to a boil. Stir constantly. Go very slowly as maple syrup tends to boil over and caramelize. Reduce heat immediately and cook for about 3 minutes. Remove from heat and add the chocolate mixture. Whisk in eggs, 1 at a time, and then add the maple whisky and pecans. Pour into the pie shell and bake.

Temperature: 350°F (180°C)

Baking Time: 50 minutes, insert knife to test if the pie is done

Garnish the pie with Coffee Maple Whipped Cream.

Coffee Maple Whipped Cream

1 cup	whipping cream	250 mL
1 tsp.	instant coffee dissolved in 2 tbsp. (30 mL) boiling water	5 mL
1 tbsp.	maple whisky	15 mL
¼ cup	maple syrup	60 mL

Whip the cream until it begins to stiffen. Add the dissolved instant coffee, maple whisky and maple syrup and beat until stiff. Place the whipping cream in a piping bag and decorate the pie.

Maple Nanaimo Bars

This three-layered bar has become famous across Canada. Named after a city in British Columbia, it can be found in any coffee chain, bakery or good kitchen across the country. In British Columbia, the maple trees are different than in Eastern Canada and the United States. Their leaves aren't just big, they are huge. Hence the name, the broadleaf maple. The trees are stunning in their beauty, as are all maples. It is a gift to see them at any time of the year. This recipe is a variation in that it marries the sap of the eastern tree with the creation of this Vancouver Island city.

Maple Coconut Pecan Base:

½ cup	soft unsalted butter	125 mL
¼ cup	maple syrup	60 mL
¼ cup	Dutch cocoa	60 mL
1 tbsp.	maple whisky	15 mL
1	egg	1
2 cups	graham wafer crumbs	500 mL
1 cup	sweet coconut	250 mL
½ cup	chopped pecans	125 mL

Custard Filling:

½ cup	unsalted butter, melted	125 mL
¼ cup	custard powder	60 mL
½ cup	whole milk	125 mL
2 cups	icing sugar	500 mL

Chocolate Topping:

3 cups	semisweet Dutch OR Belgian chocolate tempered*	750 mL
2 tbsp.	unsalted butter	30 mL

M*aple Nanaimo Bars*
(continued)

To make the base, place the soft butter, maple syrup, cocoa, maple whisky and egg in the top of a double boiler. Mix thoroughly and heat over low heat to melt the butter.

In a separate bowl, mix the graham wafer crumbs, coconut and pecans. Pour the butter and maple syrup mixture over the graham wafer mixture and stir well. Pat into a 9 x 13" (23 x 33 cm) greased pan.

To make the filling, combine the butter, custard powder and milk. Beat in the icing sugar and mix thoroughly. Spread the filling over the base. Set aside to cool.

Melt the chocolate and butter together in the top of a double boiler. Pour and spread the melted chocolate over the custard layer.

Refrigerate the Nanaimo Bars overnight and cut them into squares the next day.

Yield: 24 to 36 squares

Calories: About 6,000 per slice but, hell, you could be dead tomorrow.

* See chocolate tempering information on page 148.

157

Chocolate Coconut Haystacks

When I was a child, my mama used to make haystacks almost every week. To keep us kids going, she baked almost constantly. Thankfully, we weren't the video generation so we never gained weight. We just ran it off playing in the woods, barns, sloughs, fields, and on and around the railway right-of-way.

Today, my son Matthew takes these to work because, as he says, "haystacks travel well".

4 cups	flaked, sweetened coconut	1 L
1 cup	maple syrup	250 mL
1 cup	icing sugar	250 mL
½ cup	unsalted butter	125 mL
3 tbsp.	maple cream liqueur	45 mL
11 oz.	semisweet Dutch OR Belgian chocolate, chopped	325 g

Combine the coconut, maple syrup, sugar, butter and maple cream liqueur in a large bowl. Set aside.

Temper the chocolate in a double boiler, always being careful to keep any water from mixing with the chocolate. Let the chocolate cool.

Mix the cooled chocolate with the coconut mixture and drop by tablespoonfuls (15 mL) onto waxed paper on a cookie sheet. Refrigerate for 3 to 4 hours.

Yield: 30 to 40 haystacks, depending on how high you pile the hay

Maple Chocolate Chip Cookies

These cookies are just the best comfort food that you can imagine. Remember to use only Dutch or Belgian chocolate for best results. An inferior chocolate will spoil the excellence of the recipe.

1¼ cups	unsalted butter	300 mL
1 cup	granulated sugar	250 mL
1 cup	maple sugar OR maple syrup	250 mL
3	eggs	3
1 tbsp.	maple syrup liqueur	15 mL
2 cups	all-purpose flour	500 mL
¾ cup	Dutch cocoa	175 mL
1½ tsp.	baking soda	7 mL
½ tsp.	salt	2 mL
1 cup	chopped pecans	250 mL
2 cups	semisweet Dutch OR Belgian chocolate chips	500 mL

Cream the butter, sugar and maple syrup or sugar in a large bowl. Beat in eggs and maple syrup liqueur.

In a separate bowl, mix the flour, cocoa, baking soda and salt. Gradually incorporate the flour mixture into the butter and sugar mixture. Add the pecans and chocolate chips. Drop the dough by tablespoonfuls (15 mL) onto ungreased cookie sheets.

Temperature: 350°F (180°C)

Baking Time: 8 to 10 minutes

Yield: 4 dozen really small cookies or 2 dozen presentable size

Note: If you have problems with dark edges on the cookies, remember that maple syrup will caramelize more quickly than white or cane sugar. Simply reduce the oven temperature by 25°F (15°C) and add 2 minutes to your baking time.

Maple Devil's Food Cake

There was a time when many people thought that if a food was very, very rich and good, then it was sinful to eat. About 100 years ago, the concept of a rich, delicious chocolate cake was thought to be so bad that it had to be evil . . . hence the name, "devil's food". Today, many people feel guilty when they eat something this good, so nothing has really changed. I say, "Bring it on and enjoy it!"

½ cup	maple syrup	125 mL
¼ cup	water	60 mL
¾ cup	Dutch cocoa	175 mL
½ cup	buttermilk	125 mL
1 tsp.	maple syrup liqueur	5 mL
¾ cup	unsalted butter	175 mL
2 cups	dark brown sugar	500 mL
4	eggs	4
2¾ cups	cake flour	675 mL
2 tsp.	baking powder	10 mL
1 cup	shaved semisweet Dutch or Belgian chocolate	250 mL

Heat maple syrup and water in a saucepan and simmer briefly. Do NOT boil. Gradually add the maple syrup and water mixture to the cocoa and mix completely. Add buttermilk and maple syrup liqueur. Set aside.

In a separate bowl, beat the butter until it is light and fluffy. Add the sugar and incorporate completely. Add the 4 eggs, 1 at a time, mixing thoroughly.

In a large bowl, combine the cake flour and the baking powder. Add the buttermilk mixture and the butter and sugar mixture on an alternating basis, being careful not to over mix.

Use 2, 9" (23 cm) round cake pans with 2" (5 cm) sides. Thoroughly grease and flour each of the cake pans and pour half of the batter into each pan. Sprinkle the top of each cake with ½ cup (125 mL) of the shaved Dutch chocolate.

Temperature: 350°F (180°C)

Baking Time: 20 to 25 minutes

Frost with Maple Cappuccino Frosting, page 161, and garnish with edible flowers (violets, rose petals, etc.).

Serves: 10 to 12

Maple Cappuccino Frosting

This is somewhat like Seven Minute Frosting in texture. When I was a small child, I moved into town from the country and was invited to a birthday party where the cake had frosting similar to this. It probably says something about my personality in that all I remember about that party was the cake.

1	envelope unflavoured gelatin (¼ oz./7 g)	1
¼ cup	cold water	60 mL
½ cup	maple sugar	125 mL
2 tbsp.	instant coffee	30 mL
2 cups	whipping cream	500 mL
½ cup	chopped semisweet Dutch chocolate	125 mL

Using a small saucepan, sprinkle the gelatin over the water. Stir constantly for about a minute and then turn the heat to low and stir for another 3 to 4 minutes. Add the maple sugar and instant coffee and stir for another 3 minutes, until completely mixed. Stir in the chocolate and mix well. Remove the maple/chocolate mixture from the heat and chill slightly.

In a separate bowl, beat the whipping cream. Beat until almost stiff. Beat in the cooled maple/chocolate mixture. Beat until stiff. Allow the frosting to chill somewhat before icing the cake.

Yield: sufficient frosting for a 9" (23 cm), 2-layer cake

Vermont Maple Fudge Cake

It seems fair to say that the state of Vermont is one of the largest producers of maple syrup and, accordingly, it should have a cake named after it.

⅔ cup	dark Dutch chocolate	150 mL
1⅓ cups	maple syrup	325 mL
1¾ cups	cake flour	425 mL
1½ tsp.	baking soda	7 mL
1½ tsp.	salt	7 mL
⅔ cup	unsalted butter	150 mL
4	eggs, at room temperature	4
¾ cup	whole milk	175 mL
1 tsp.	maple cream liqueur	5 mL
1 cup	chopped macadamia nuts	250 mL

Temper the chocolate in the top section of a double boiler according to the tempering directions on page 148. Very slowly, stir half of the maple syrup into the melted chocolate. Cool.

Mix the flour, baking soda and salt in a separate bowl. In another bowl, cream the butter and slowly add the remaining maple syrup. Incorporate completely, then beat in the eggs, 1 at a time. Start adding the flour mixture slowly, along with the milk, and then add the chocolate mixture and the maple cream liqueur. Stir in the nuts.

Pour the batter into 2 greased and floured 9" (23 cm) round cake pans.

Temperature: 350°F (180°C)

Baking Time: 30 minutes

Ice this cake with Maple Butter Icing, page 143. If this is a splendid occasion, top the cake with chocolate maple leaves or chocolate butterflies, see the instructions on page 149.

Serves: 8 to 10

Pictured on page 140.

Maple Cream Chocolate Torte

The Europeans invented the miracle of the chocolate sandwich. In many European countries it is just fine if you show up at school with chocolate spread sandwiches in your lunch. It is a given that the chocolate won't be grainy or waxy. So it makes sense that you could go up a notch and take the following cake for lunch, but you might have to skip the booze if you are in grade school.

⅔ cup	unsalted butter	150 mL
¾ cup	maple syrup	175 mL
1 tbsp.	finely grated lemon zest	15 mL
1 tbsp.	finely grated orange zest	15 mL
6	eggs, separated	6
6 oz.	Dutch OR Belgian chocolate	170 g
1 cup	cake/pastry flour	250 mL
⅓ cup	maple cream liqueur	75 mL
	Coffee Maple Whipped Cream OR	
	Maple Butter Icing, see below	
	chocolate-covered coffee beans (optional)	

Beat the butter, maple syrup, lemon zest and orange zest together in a large bowl until smooth. Add the egg yolks, 1 at a time, and continue beating until they are well incorporated.

Melt the chocolate in a double boiler (see notes on melting chocolate on page 148). Stir the slightly cooled chocolate into the egg mixture.

In a separate bowl, beat the egg whites until they are very stiff and shiny. Gently fold the egg whites into the chocolate mixture. Add the flour and mix gently.

Pour the batter into 2 greased and floured 1½ x 8" (4 x 20 cm) round cake pans.

Temperature: 375°F (190°C)

Baking Time: 45 to 50 minutes

After the cakes have cooled, cut them horizontally into 2. You now have 4 cakes. Sprinkle the maple cream liqueur on each surface prior to covering with Coffee Maple Whipped Cream, page 155, or Maple Butter Icing, page 143. Decorate with chocolate-covered coffee beans, if you wish.

Serves: 8

Andy's Mile-High Maple Chocolate Cake

My nephew Andrew baked a chocolate cake with green icing when he was about ten years old. It looked like it had been run over by a freight train but it tasted fantastic. Andy always kept trying. It's thirty-two years later and he's still the same. This is his cake, just taller.

2¼ cups	cake flour	550 mL
1¾ cups	maple syrup	425 mL
⅓ cup	Dutch cocoa	75 mL
1¾ tsp.	baking powder	9 mL
1¾ tsp.	baking soda	9 mL
1¼ tsp.	salt	6 mL
4	large eggs at room temperature	4
1 cup	whole milk	250 mL
½ cup	heavy cream	125 mL
⅔ cup	unsalted butter, softened	150 mL
1 tbsp.	maple whisky OR maple cream liqueur	15 mL
1¼ cups	boiling water	300 mL

Combine the dry ingredients in a large mixing bowl. Add the eggs, milk, cream, softened butter and maple whisky. Beat on medium speed for 2 minutes. Stir in the boiling water and mix well. At this stage, the batter will be quite thin.

Pour the batter into 4 greased and well-floured 1½ x 8" (4 x 20 cm) round cake pans.

Temperature: 350°F (180°C)

Baking Time: 35 to 40 minutes, or until a cake tester inserted in the centre of the cake comes out clean.

Serves: 10

Note: Ice with a lovely Maple Butter Icing, page 143. Remember, for such a large cake, you might need a double portion of icing. It's better to have a lot of icing because you don't want to look cheap.

Resource Section

CLEARY'S MAPLE PRODUCTS
574 Notre-Dame North
P.O. Box 74
Robertsonville, Québec
Canada G0N 1L0

Website: www.cleary.ca
        www.clearysmapleproducts.com
E-mail: info@cleary.ca

Jo-Ann Cleary,
   Sales & Marketing
Telephone: 1-877-77-MAPLE
           (Canada & USA)
           1-450-923-6019
           (worldwide)
FAX: 1-877-7-ERABLE
           (Canada & USA)
           1-450-923-0966
           (worldwide)

ÉRABLIÈRE LA COULÉE D'ABBOTSFORD SUGARBUSH INC.
780 Fisk Street
St-Paul-d'Abbotsford, Québec
Canada J0E 1A0

E-mail: lacoulee_sugarbush@videotron.ca

Sylvie Chagnon, Vice-President,
   Sales & Marketing
Telephone: 1-450-379-5364
FAX: 1-450-379-9793

THE GREAT CANADIAN FUDGE COMPANY
20779 Lougheed Hwy.
Maple Ridge, British Columbia
Canada V2X 2R2

Website: www.greatcanadianfudge.com
E-mail: greatcanadianfudge@telus.net

Jeremy Stevens, President
Telephone: 1-604-463-2440
FAX: 1-604-463-8455
Toll-Free: 1-888-462-4447

JAKEMAN'S MAPLE PRODUCTS
R.R. #1,
454414 Trillium Line
Beachville, Ontario
Canada N0J 1A0

E-mail: bob@themaplestore.com

Bob Jakeman, President
Telephone: 1-519-539-1366
FAX: 1-519-421-2469

Resource Section

🍁 **KITTLING RIDGE LTD.**

Website: www.KittlingRidge.com

Tim Burrows,
Vice-President of Sales
Telephone: 1-905-945-9225
                   Extension 13
FAX: 1-905-945-4330

Manufacturers of maple cream liqueur and other products.

🍁 **MAPLE LEAF DISTILLERS**
235 McPhillips Street
Winnipeg, Manitoba
Canada R3E 2K3

Scott Wilson,
Director of Sales

Website: www.mapleleafdistillers.com
E-mail: mapleleaf@ilos.net
    Manufacturers of maple syrup liqueur and maple cream liqueur.

🍁 **SMOKEY KETTLE MAPLE COMPANY LIMITED**
P.O. Box 117
623 South Service Rd. Unit #8
Grimsby, Ontario
Canada L3M 4G1

Peter Heersink,
Vice-President
Telephone: 1-905-643-9215
FAX: 1-905-643-9216
Toll-Free: 1-800-461-1752
          (North American)

E-mail: smokeykettle.maplesyrup@sympatico.ca

🍁 **TURKEY HILL SUGARBUSH LTD.**
P.O. Box 160
10 Waterloo Street
Waterloo, Québec
Canada J0E 2N0

Michael S.L. Herman,
President
Telephone: 1-450-539-4822
FAX: 1-450-539-1561

E-mail: turkeyhillsugarbush@qc.aibn.com

Index

A

Allan's Dutch Apple Baby 16
Allison Duthie's Maple Rice Experience 54
Ambrosia 92
Andy's Mile-High Maple Chocolate Cake .. 164
Apple Blueberry Pie with Maple Sugar
    Crust 128
Apple Crisp Pie, Maple 133
August Garden Salad 42

B

Baked Beans, Maple 49
Baked Maple Squash 47
Baking and Cooking with Maple Sugar
    and Maple Syrup 122
Balsamic Maple Dressing 42
Banana Bread, Maple 25
Bananas Flambé 99
Barbecued Salmon 66
Beef with Portobello Mushrooms &
    Maple Whisky Sauce 77

Beverages, Breakfasts & Breads
Beverages
Irish Canadian Coffee 11
Maple Mango Smoothie 10
Maple Summer Sangria 10

Breakfasts
Allan's Dutch Apple Baby 16
Cornmeal Maple Waffles 20
Cornmeal Waffles with Bacon 20
Crunchy Maple Cranberry Granola 12
Johnny's Skinny Pancakes 15
Magnificent Maple Granola 13
Maple Sugar Waffles 19
Raymond's Hurry-Up/Wake-Up Maple
    Bananas 21
Raymond's Mac Crêpes 14

Breads
Blueberry Maple Muffins 22
Carrot Muffins, Maple 137
Cleary 's Maple Chip Muffins 24
Maple Banana Bread 25
Maple Blueberry Bread 26
Maple Coffee Cake 28
Maple Glory Muffins 22
Maple Mango Muffins 23
Pumpkin Maple Breakfast Bread 27

Blueberry Bread, Maple 26
Blueberry Maple Crunch 102
Blueberry Maple Ice Cream 92
Blueberry Maple Muffins 22
Blueberry Pie 127
Blueberry Trifle, Maple Cream 103
Boiled Maple Icing 144
Brown Bean Soup, Maple 36

Butter Icing, Maple 143
Butter Tarts, Maple 124

C

Cakes, Cookies & Squares
Cakes
Andy's Mile-High Maple Chocolate
    Cake 164
Chocolate Maple Mousse Cheesecake ... 152
Maple Apple Cake 141
Maple Cream Chocolate Torte 163
Maple Devil's Food Cake 160
Maple Heaven Carrot Cake 137
Maple Pound Cake 138
Maple Syrup Cake 142
Vermont Maple Fudge Cake 162

Cookies
Maple Chocolate Chip Cookies 159
Raisin Oatmeal Maple Cookies 146

Icings
Boiled Maple Icing 144
Coffee Maple Whipped Cream 155
Maple Butter Icing 143
Maple Cappuccino Frosting 161
Maple Chocolate Butter Icing 143

Squares
Maple Nanaimo Bars 156
Maple Pecan Squares 145

Candies
Chocolate Coconut Haystacks 158
Crunchy Maple Jungle Bark 111
Manitoba Maple Creams 109
Maple Chocolate Crisps 114
Maple Macadamia Chocolate Fudge 113
Maple Nut Brittle 110
Maple Popcorn 115
Maple Syrup Fudge Sauce 116
Maple Turtles 112

Canadian Maple Stew 78
Canadian Maple Wild Rice 55
Cappuccino Mousse, Maple 117
Carrot Cake, Maple Heaven 137
Carrot Muffins, Maple 137
Carrots, Leek & Cauliflower, Maple 46
Cheese Casserole, Maple 62
Chicken Parisienne, Maple 76
Chicken Stock 38
Chili, Maple 79

Chocolate
Andy's Mile-High Maple Chocolate Cake . 164
Chocolate Butterflies 149
Chocolate Butter Icing, Maple 143
Chocolate Coconut Haystacks 158
Chocolate Chip Cookies, Maple 159
Chocolate Cups 149
Chocolate Leaves 149
Chocolate Maple Mousse Cheesecake 152
Chocolate Maple Pears 98

167

Chocolate (continued)

Chocolate Maple Sauce 98
Chocolate Mousse, Maple 150
Chocolate Mousse Pie, Maple 154
Chocolate Shells 149
Chocolate Torte, Maple Cream 163
Maple Cappuccino Frosting 161
Maple Chocolate Chip Cookies 159
Maple Chocolate Crisps 114
Maple Chocolate Mousse Pie 154
Maple Cream Chocolate Torte 163
Maple Devil's Food Cake 160
Maple Macadamia Chocolate Fudge 113
Maple Macadamia Mousse 151
Maple Nanaimo Bars 156
Maple Pecan Chocolate Pie 155
Maple Turtles 112
Tempering Chocolate 148
Vermont Maple Fudge Cake 162

Cilantro Dressing, Maple 41
Cleary 's Maple Chip Muffins 24
Coffee Maple Whipped Cream 155
Coffee Cake, Maple 28
Coleslaw, Maple 43
Cream and Mushroom Scallops, Maple 63
Cream Blueberry Trifle, Maple 103
Cream of Carrot Soup, Maple 32
Creamy Maple Corn Soup 33
Creamy Mushroom Soup 34
Crab Newburg, Maple 62
Crème Brûlée, Maple 118
Crêpes Maple Melba 100
Crunchy Maple Cranberry Granola 12
Crunchy Maple Jungle Bark 111
Custard, Maple 118

D

Deep Dutch Maple Apple Pie 132
Dilled Arctic Char with Saskatoon Berry
  Sauce 65
Devil's Food Cake, Maple 160
Dilled Salmon, Maple 67

F

Fatoosh, Maple 41

Fruit

Ambrosia 92
Apple Blueberry Pie 128
Bananas Flambé 99
Blueberry Maple Crunch 102
Blueberry Maple Ice Cream 92
Blueberry Pie 127
Chocolate Maple Pears 98
Crêpes Maple Melba 100
Deep Dutch Maple Apple Pie 132
Fruit Barbecue Sauce, Maple 82
Larissa's Maple Tropical Salad 90
Mango Maple Meringues 94
Maple Apple Cake 141

Maple Apple Crisp Pie 133
Maple Cream Blueberry Trifle 103
Maple Macadamia Granny Crunch 101
Maple Macadamia Ice Cream 93
Maple Mango Cheesecake 104
Maple Moon Rhubarb Pie 131
Maple Mudslide 95
Maple Peach Pie 130
Maple Raisin Pie 134
Maple Whisky Peaches 98
Papa's Maple Apples 97
Peter Stuyvesant Maple Fruit Salad 91
Raymond's Hurry-Up/Wake-Up Maple
  Bananas 21
Strawberry Maple Cream 93
Strawberry Maple Syrup Parfait 96

Fruit Barbecue Sauce, Maple 82

G

Ginger Chicken, Maple 72
Ginger Crumb Crust 104
Gouda Soup, Maple 35

H

Ham and Pineapple Casserole, Maple 84
Ham, Maple-Glazed 83

I

Irish Canadian Coffee 11

J

Johnny's Skinny Pancakes 15

L

Larissa's Maple Tropical Salad 90
Lemon Glaze, Maple 26
Lobster and Avocado Salad with Maple
  Dressing 44

M

Macadamia Chocolate Fudge, Maple 114
Macadamia Granny Crunch, Maple 101
Macadamia Ice Cream, Maple 93
Macadamia Mousse, Maple 151
Magnificent Maple Granola 13

Main Course Dishes

Maple Cheese Casserole 62
Beef
Beef with Portobello Mushrooms & Maple
  Whisky Sauce 77
Canadian Maple Stew 78
Maple Chili 79
Maple Meatballs in Cream Sauce 80
Pork
Maple Ham and Pineapple Casserole 84
Maple-Glazed Ham 83
Marinated Maple Spareribs 81
Matthew's Maple Fruit Spareribs 82

Poultry

Maple Chicken Parisienne 76
Maple Ginger Chicken 72
Maple Sambal Chicken 73
Sweet and Sour Maple Chicken 74
Sweet and Sour Maple Chicken Wings . . 75

Seafood & Shellfish

Barbecued Salmon 66
Dilled Arctic Char with Saskatoon
   Berry Sauce 65
John's Maple Salmon Loaf 68
Mango Maple Tiger Shrimp 64
Maple Crab Newburg 62
Maple Cream and Mushroom Scallops . . . 63
Maple Dilled Salmon 67
Maple Salmon Mousse 71

Mango Cheesecake, Maple 104
Mango Maple Meringues 94
Mango Maple Tiger Shrimp 64
Mango Smoothie, Maple 10
Mango Spinach Salad, Maple 39
Manitoba Maple Creams 110
Maple Almond Glaze 104
Maple Apple Cake 141
Maple Butter Icing 143
Maple Cappuccino Frosting 161
Maple Chocolate Crisps 114
Maple Cinnamon Sauce 46
Maple Macadamia Mousse 151
Maple Meringue Topping 125
Maple Moon Rhubarb Pie 131
Maple Mustard Dressing 43
Maple Nut Brittle 110
Maple Pecan Chocolate Pie 155
Maple Popcorn 115
Maple Sugar Crust 128
Maple Sugar Pie (Tarte au Sucre) 126
Maple Sugar Tarts 126
Maple Syrup Cake 142
Maple Syrup Fudge Sauce 116
Maple Syrup Pie 125
Maple Whisky Peaches 98
Marinated Maple Spareribs 81
Matthew's Maple Fruit Spareribs 82
Meatballs in Cream Sauce, Maple 80
Meringues, Mango Maple 94
Meringue Topping 125
Molly's Maple Carrots 45
Mudslide, Maple 95
Muffins, Maple Glory 22
Muffins, Maple Mango 23
Mushroom Soup, Maple 34

N

Nanaimo Bars, Maple 156
Nasturtium Maple Dressing 44
Never-Fail Pie Crust 124

O

Oatmeal Cinnamon Crust 102
Oven-Roasted Maple Onion Potatoes 39

P

Papa's Maple Apples 97
Peach Blueberry Pie, Maple 130
Peach Pie, Maple 130
Peaches, Maple Whisky 98
Pecan Chocolate Pie, Maple 155
Pecan Squares, Maple 145
Peter Stuyvesant Maple Fruit Salad 91

Pies, Tarts, Pie Doughs & Crusts

Pies

Apple Blueberry Pie with Maple Sugar
   Crust 128
Blueberry Pie 127
Deep Dutch Maple Apple Pie 132
Maple Apple Crisp Pie 133
Maple Butter Tarts 124
Maple Chocolate Mousse Pie 154
Maple Meringue Topping 125
Maple Moon Rhubarb Pie 131
Maple Peach Blueberry Pie 130
Maple Peach Pie 130
Maple Pecan Chocolate Pie 155
Maple Raisin Pie 134
Maple Sugar Crust 128
Maple Sugar Pie (Tarte au Sucre) 126
Maple Sugar Tarts 126
Maple Syrup Pie 125
Never-Fail Pie Crust 124
Québec Maple Sugar Pie 126

Pie Dough & Crusts

Chocolate Maple Crust 152
Ginger Crumb Crust 104
Maple Sugar Crust 128
Never-Fail Pie Crust 124
Sweet Dough 132

Pound Cake, Maple 138

Puddings

Maple Cappuccino Mousse 117
Maple Chocolate Mousse 150
Maple Crème Brûlée 118
Maple Custard 118
Maple Macadamia Mousse 151
Maple Raisin Bread Pudding 120
Maple Rice Pudding 119

Pumpkin Maple Breakfast Bread 27

Q

Québec Maple Sugar Pie 126

R

Raisin Bread Pudding, Maple 120
Raisin Oatmeal Maple Cookies 146
Raisin Pie, Maple 134
Raymond's Hurry-Up/Wake-Up Maple
   Bananas 21
Raymond's Mac Crêpes 14
Rhubarb Pie, Maple Moon 131
Rice Pudding, Maple 119

S

Salads & Salad Dressings

Salads

Ambrosia 92
August Garden Salad, The 42
Larissa's Maple Tropical Salad 90
Lobster and Avocado Salad with Maple
   Dressing 44
Maple Coleslaw 43
Maple Fatoosh 41
Maple Mango Spinach Salad 39
Peter Stuyvesant Maple Fruit Salad 91
Summer Evening Salad 40

Salad Dressings

Balsamic Maple Dressing 42
Maple Cilantro Dressing 41
Maple Mustard Dressing 43
Maple Raspberry Vinaigrette 40
Maple Vinaigrette 39
Nasturtium Maple Dressing 44

Salmon Loaf, John's Maple 68
Salmon Mousse, Maple 71
Sambal Chicken, Maple 73
Saskatoon Berry Sauce 56
Saskatoon Maple Barbecue Glaze 58
Sangria, Maple Summer 10

Sauces, Marinades & Glazes

Chocolate Maple Sauce 98
Maple Almond Glaze 104
Maple Cinnamon Sauce 46
Maple Fruit Barbecue Sauce 82
Maple Lemon Glaze 26
Maple Sweet and Sour Sauce 75
Maple Syrup Fudge Sauce 116
Maple Teriyaki Marinade 81
Maple Whisky Sauce 55, 77, 120
Saskatoon Berry Sauce 56
Saskatoon Maple Barbecue Glaze 58
Thanksgiving Cranberries 56
Tropical Maple Syrup Glaze 57

Scalloped Potatoes, Maple 53

Soups

Chicken Stock 38
Creamy Maple Corn Soup 33
Creamy Mushroom Soup 34
Maple Brown Bean Soup 36
Maple Cream of Carrot Soup 32
Maple Gouda Soup 35
Maple Mushroom Soup 34
Vegetable Stock 37

Squares

Maple Nanaimo Bars 156
Maple Pecan Squares 145
Strawberry Maple Cream 93
Strawberry Maple Syrup Parfait 96
Summer Evening Salad 40
Sweet and Sour Maple Chicken 74
Sweet and Sour Maple Chicken Wings 75
Sweet and Sour Sauce, Maple 75
Sweet Dough 132

T

Tempering Chocolate 148
Teriyaki Marinade, Maple 81
Thanksgiving Cranberries 56
Tropical Maple Syrup Glaze 57
Turkey Hill Red Cabbage 45
Turnip Purée with Bacon, Maple 48
Turtles, Maple 112

V

Vegetable Stock 37

Vegetables

Allison Duthie's Maple Rice Experience ... 54
Baked Maple Squash 47
Canadian Maple Wild Rice 55
Maple Baked Beans 49
Maple Carrots, Leek & Cauliflower 46
Maple Scalloped Potatoes 53
Maple Turnip Purée with Bacon 48
Maple Winter Vegetables 46
Molly's Maple Carrots 45
Oven-Roasted Maple Onion Potatoes 50
Turkey Hill Red Cabbage 45

Vermont Maple Fudge Cake 162
Vinaigrette, Maple 39
Vinaigrette, Maple Raspberry 40

W

Waffles, Cornmeal Maple 20
Waffles, Cornmeal with Bacon 20
Waffles, Maple Sugar 19
Whipped Cream, Coffee Maple 155
Whipped Cream, Maple 19, 28, 141
Whisky Sauce, Maple 55, 77, 120
Winter Vegetables, Maple 46

Share *Maple Moon*™ with a friend

Maple Moon™ – number of books _____ x $18.95 = $ _____

Let's Go Dutch® – number of books _____ x $19.95 = $ _____

Shipping and handling charge _____ = $ __4.50__

Subtotal _____ = $ _____

In Canada add 7% GST OR 15% HST where applicable = $ _____

Total enclosed _____ = $ _____

U.S. and international orders payable in U.S. funds.

Price is subject to change.

NAME: _____

STREET: _____

CITY: _____ PROV./STATE _____

COUNTRY: _____ POSTAL CODE/ZIP _____

TELEPHONE:_____ FAX: _____

Please make cheque or money order payable to:

Maple Moon Publishing
Suite 101, 2212 – 34 Avenue SW
Fax: (403) 299-5467   **Calgary, Alberta**
E-mail: query@telusplanet.net   **Canada   T2T 2C6**

For fundraising or volume purchase prices, contact Maple Moon™ Publishing.

Please allow 3-4 weeks for delivery.

Let's Go Dutch®

by Johanna (van der Zeijst) Bates

Back in Print! Taste the legendary flavours of Dutch chocolate and pastry. Delight in the wonderful stories and recipes surrounding Saint Nicholas and the Christmas season. Enjoy the hearty soups and main courses, including splendid game and seafood recipes. A fabulous Indonesian section introduces you to the exotic flavours of the far east. Historical notes, anecdotes and warm family memories complete this treasury of Dutch cooking.

Retail $19.95   7" x 10"
224 pages   10 colour photographs
ISBN 0-919845-54-1

 172